THE VIKING RUNES *Traditional Meanings*

ᛗ	the Self	Man, the Human Race
ᚷ	Partnership	A Gift, Offerings from the Gods or from Chiefs to Loyal Followers
ᚠ	Signals	God, the God Loki, Mouth (source of Divine Utterances), Rivermouth
ᛟ	Retreat	Property or Inherited Possessions, also Native Land, Home
ᚢ	Strength	Strength, Sacrificial Animal, the Aurochs (*bos primigenius*), species of wild ox
ᚲ	Initiation	Uncertain Meaning, a Secret Matter (Rune of Mystery)
ᚾ	Constraint	Need, Necessity, Constraint, Cause of Human Sorrow, Lessons, Hardship
ᛜ	Fertility	Ing, the Legendary Hero, later a God
ᛇ	Defense	Yew-tree, a Bow Made of Yew, Rune Magic, Avertive Powers: Runic Calendars or "Primstaves"
ᛉ	Protection	Protection, Defense, the Elk, Sedge or Eelgrass
ᚡ	Possessions	Cattle, Goods, the Vital Community Wealth
ᚹ	Joy	Joy, also in *Cynewulf's* Runic Passages, Absence of Suffering & Sorrow
ᛞ	Harvest	Year, Harvest, A Fruitful Year
ᚴ	Opening	Torch, Skiff, Ulcer, Associated with Cult of the Goddess Nerthus
ᛏ	Warrior	Victory in Battle, a Guiding Planet or Star, the God Tīw
ᛒ	Growth	Birch Tree, Associated with Fertility Cults, Rebirth, New Life
ᛖ	Movement	Horse, Associated with the Course of the Sun
ᚱ	Flow	Water, Sea, a Fertility Source (See Grendel's Mere in *Beowulf*)
ᚺ	Disruption	Hail, Sleet, Natural Forces that Damage
ᚱ	Journey	A Riding, a Journey: Refers to the Soul After Death, Journey Charm
ᚦ	Gateway	Giant, Demon, Thorn
ᛉ	Breakthrough	Day, God's Light, Prosperity and Fruitfulness
ᛁ	Standstill	Ice, Freezing, in the *Prose Edda* the Frost-giant Ymir is Born of Ice
ᛋ	wholeness	The Sun
☐	the unknowable	The Rune of Destiny

The
BOOK
Of
RUNES

*To lend courage to virtue
and ardor to truth . . .*
Dr. Samuel Johnson

The
BOOK
Of
RUNES

*A Handbook for the Use of
an Ancient Oracle:
The Viking Runes*

Ralph Blum

ST. MARTIN'S PRESS
NEW YORK

Illustrations by Jancis Salerno

THE BOOK OF RUNES. Copyright © 1982 by Ralph Blum. All
rights reserved. Printed in the United States of America. No
part of this book may be used or reproduced in any manner
whatsoever without written permission except in the case of
brief quotations embodied in critical articles or reviews. For
information, address St. Martin's Press, 175 Fifth Avenue,
New York, N.Y. 10010.

Design by Deborah Daly

Library of Congress Cataloging in Publication Data

Blum, Ralph, 1932–
    The book of runes.

    Includes index.
    1. Runes—Miscellanea.   2. Oracles.   I. Title.
BF1779.R86B58   1983   133.3'3   83-10998
ISBN 0-312-09001-3 (package only)
ISBN 0-312-09002-1 (book only)
First published in the U.S. in 1982 by Oracle Books.

CONTENTS

*This book is lovingly dedicated
to
Margaret Mead*

PREFACE

The Runes as described here are healing, merciful Runes; they will do you no harm. Learn their language and let them speak to you. Play with the possibility that they can provide "a mirror for the magic of our Knowing Selves," a means of communication with the knowledge of our subconscious minds.

Remember that you are consulting an Oracle rather than having your fortune told. An Oracle does not give you instruction as to what to do next, nor does it predict future events. An Oracle points your attention towards those hidden fears and motivations that will shape your future by their unfelt presence within each present moment. Once seen and recognized, these factors become absorbed into the realm of choice. Oracles do not absolve you of the responsibility for selecting your future, but rather direct your attention towards those inner choices that may be the most important elements in determining that future.

How can random selection of marked stones tell you anything about yourself? Perhaps these Rune interpretations are simply so evocative that each contains *some* point which can be accepted as relevant to *some* part of what is happening at the limits of consciousness any day, any time, to anyone. That is the easiest possibility to accept from a strictly scientific standpoint. Nevertheless, my own play with these Runes has shown coincidence piled upon coincidence and an apparently consistent "appropriateness" in each Rune reading which is difficult to explain by the mechanism I have just described.

Can there be other factors that distort the expected randomness of Rune selection so as to provide a language by which the subconscious makes itself and its expectations known? For myself, I maintain an open mind, reminding myself that observations should not be discounted simply because their underlying mechanisms have not yet been satisfactorily explained.

So go ahead. Try out these Runes. See if this Oracle can mirror your subconscious process, but remember that such a link may take practice to develop. The Rune interpretations offered here come from the meditations of a gentle, healing mind. They will speak to you of change and growth. The only negativity you will find here relates to the blockage of appropriate growth, while all the positive aspects are transcendent, transforming and lead to breakthroughs. The subconscious you will encounter here is not a fearsome beast in need of obedience training. It is the inner seeker-after-truth who must be helped to save us from ourselves.

Dr. Martin D. Rayner
Professor of Physiology
University of Hawaii School of Medicine

Odin on the Yggdrasil,
or World Tree,
Spies the Runes

HAVAMAL
"THE SPEECH OF THE HIGH ONE"

I know I hung on that windy tree,
Swung there for nine long nights,
Wounded by my own blade,
Bloodied for Odin,
Myself an offering to myself:
Bound to the tree
That no man knows
Whither the roots of it run.

None gave me bread,
None gave me drink.
Down to the deepest depths I peered
Until I spied the Runes.
With a roaring cry I seized them up,
Then dizzy and fainting, I fell.

Well-being I won
And wisdom too.
I grew and took joy in my growth:
From a word to a word
I was led to a word,
From a deed to another deed.

From the Old Norse
The Poetic Edda (ca. A.D. 1200)

INTRODUCTION

Few people today have even heard the word "Runes." Among those of Scandinavian descent and among readers of Tolkien, yes, a light goes on. But that's about the extent of it. An ancient alphabetic script each of whose letters possessed a meaningful name as well as a signifying sound, Runes were employed for poetry, for inscriptions and divination, yet never evolved as a spoken language. Next to nothing has been written about Runes as a contemporary Oracle.

The midwifing of alphabets and Oracles is a strange and mysterious transaction. Both the alphabetical ordering and the letter interpretations found in *The Book of Runes* are non-conventional. Yet there is historical support for such flexibility. The great Danish scholar L. F. A. Wimmer regarded the creation of the runic alphabet as the work of one unknown individual (rather than as an evolutionary process), much as Bishop Wulfila created the Gothic alphabet for the West Goths of the fourth century.

Moreover, the interpretations of the Runes as used for divination are lost to us. While *legomonism*—the passing on of sacred knowledge through initiation—was, no doubt, practiced among Rune Masters of old, their secrets were not recorded or, if recorded, did not survive.

My first attempt at writing a handbook for the use of the Runes as an Oracle included seventy-three pages of history, philology and archeology. But then my way of learning a subject is to research it, digest it, synthesize and write it and, finally, with the firm hand of a friendly editor guiding my own, to cut the text severely. For support and courage in this not inconsiderable task, I gratefully thank my editor, Bronwyn Jones. Practicing self-control in limiting the contents of this book involved me in the discipline of the Spiritual Warrior, the one whose aim is always to be impeccable in his or her conduct.

It is with the Spiritual Warrior in mind at all times that I have composed *The Book of Runes*. The Spiritual Warrior is free of anxiety, radically alone, unconcerned with outcomes; he or she practices absolute trust in the struggle for awareness, and is constantly mindful that what matters is to have *a true present*. It takes a long time to grow in wisdom, to say nothing of the long time it takes to learn to think well. Following the Warrior Way is not for everyone, although it is available to all who are willing to undergo its hardships. To embark on the path is to cultivate the Witness Self, the Watcher

Within, the one who can profitably converse with the Runes.

For my own introduction to the study of Oracles I am indebted to Dr. Allan W. Anderson of the Department of Religious Studies, San Diego State University. Dr. Anderson, who has a substantial working knowledge of Sanskrit, Hebrew, Greek and Chinese, teaches a course entitled "The Oracular Tradition," in which he presents the *I Ching* as "the only systematic sacred text we possess." His influence, his spirit, his concepts* provide a unique teaching of the finest art of all—the art of self-change.

I have included at the end of *The Book of Runes* a Selected Bibliography for those who wish to press on in the study of runology. However, since to my knowledge there is in print no work having for its focus the practical application of runic wisdom for self-counseling, that is the primary purpose of this book. A second short bibliography, Guides to the Transformational Process, is included for those who have chosen to follow what Black Elk calls "the path with a heart," the path of the Spiritual Warrior.

Before beginning to write, I consulted the Runes about the timeliness of the undertaking. I drew three Runes and got *Inguz* $\diamond$, the Rune of Fertility and New Beginnings; *Nauthiz* $\uparrow$, the Rune of Necessity, Constraint and Pain; and *Dagaz* $\bowtie$, the Rune

---

*"Strive to live the ordinary life in a non-ordinary way. . . . In the spiritual life there is no momentum: you are always at the beginning."

of Breakthrough and Transformation. *The Book of Runes* was conceived in one fertile sleepless night. The constraint required for the amputation of those seventy-three pages was certainly not without pain. Yet through it all I kept mindful of a French saying, "Pain is the craft entering into the apprentice." The work itself has been a source of transformation in my own life and, through their introduction to the Runes, in the lives of many others.

All along the way, since beginning this book, there have been positive signs and omens. The final sign came as I completed the Afterword. Since the last Rune Masters lived in seventeenth-century Iceland, it seemed to me fitting to close the loop with an Icelandic blessing. In order to check the spelling of *Gud blessi thig,* the Icelandic for "God bless you," I placed a call to the Icelandic Consulate in New York. The woman who answered confirmed the spelling. When I told her what I was writing, and about my work with the Runes, she paused a long moment, then said, "My name is Sigrun. It means 'Rune of Victory.' "

ENVOI

God within me, God without,
How shall I ever be in doubt?
There is no place where I may go
And not there see God's face, not know
I am God's vision and God's ears.
So through the harvest of my years
I am the Sower and the Sown,
God's Self unfolding and God's own.

Grave stone, St. Lars Church, Linkoping,
tenth century

I

THE ORACLE
OF THE SELF

oracle, *from the Latin* oraculum, *divine announcement . . . 1. among the ancient Greeks and Romans, a) the place where, or medium by which, deities were consulted; b) the revelation or response of a medium or priest; 2. a) any person or agency believed to be in communication with a deity; b) any person of great knowledge or wisdom; c) opinions or statements of any such oracle; 3) the holy of holies of the ancient Jewish Temple.*

Webster's New World Dictionary

And the oracle he prepared in the house within, to set there the ark of the covenant of the Lord.

I Kings 6:19

The purpose of this book is to reintroduce an ancient Oracle, the Runes. Older than the New Testament, the Runes have lain fallow for more than 300 years. Akin in function to the Tarot and the Chinese *Book of Changes,* the Runes were last in current use in Iceland during the late Middle Ages. In their time they served as the *I Ching* of the Vikings. Like all true Oracles, the Runes are an instrument for tuning in to our own wisdom.

At our best, each of us is a channel through which God's wisdom flows, and we are sensitive to the inner guidance that provides us with the intuitive knowing we require. But life can be hard and difficult and we are not always clear. The channels that we are often become blocked by fears, silted up with self-doubt. We do not always hear the still small voice that is our natural inheritance. Consulting the Runes will put you in touch with your own inner guidance, with the part of you that knows everything you need to know for your life now.

Throughout *The Book of Runes* I use the term *self* to represent the little self or ego-self, and *Self* to signify the Higher or Transpersonal Self. The Runes, then, are a dowsing rod. With their help, you can locate the ground water of timely right action and undertake the one activity that has no equal: self-change. In ancient times, the Runes and their symbols were employed by warriors bent on conquest. It is my hope that the Runes, in their contemporary use, will serve the Spiritual Warrior, the one whose quest is doing battle with the self, the one whose goal is self-transformation. The *Bhagavad Gita* in chapter 6, verse 5, says it succinctly:

> *Lift up the self by the Self*
> *And don't let the self droop down,*
> *For the Self is the self's only friend*
> *And the self is the Self's only foe.*

The motto for the Runes could be the same words that were carved above the gate of the Oracle at Delphi: *Know thyself.* The Runes are a teacher. Yet for some it may be more comfortable to approach the Runes in a spirit of play. Oracles are sacred games, instruments for serious or high play, and the value of play is that it frees us from the effort of learning, frees us to learn as children learn. *The Book of Runes* is offered as a primer for oracular play.

Each of us is an Oracle, and when we pray to the Divine we are exercising our true oracular function, which is to consult the Knowing Self within. We are living in an age of radical discontinuity. The lessons come faster and faster as our souls and the universe push us into growth. Familiar waters seem suddenly perilous, alive with uncharted shoals and shifting sandbars. The old maps are outdated; we require new navigational aids. And the inescapable fact is: *you are your own cartographer now.*

If there is one prominent modern authority for the efficacy of Oracles, it is Carl Jung. He had the wisdom to see and the courage to affirm that "Theoretical considerations of cause and effect often look pale and dusty in comparison to the practical results of chance."* This means that nothing is too insignifi-

*C. G. Jung, Foreword to the *I Ching* (Princeton, N.J.: Princeton University Press, 1950).

cant to regard as a clue to guide us in right and timely action. Consulting an Oracle is a real-time event, because whatever happens in the given moment possesses what Jung calls "the quality peculiar to that moment." Consulting an Oracle places you in true present time.

Having a true present is something most of us find extremely difficult. We waste a good part of our lives dwelling on past regrets and fantasizing future disasters. In my own life, when I jog or drive long distances, I am often busy reviewing ideas, sorting schemes, going over options and opportunities. All of a sudden I catch myself at it; I realize that miles of countryside have slipped by unseen, that I am not breathing the air, not aware of the trees, the breeze, the ruts in the pavement. Nowadays, I catch myself more and more frequently, which is a beginning. The "roof-brain chatter" is being replaced with a stillness that keeps me in the *now*. The momentum is broken, the habit is broken. I have only to remember: *in the spiritual life there is no momentum, I am always at the beginning.* Each move brings us to a new beginning. Remembering this helps overcome our addiction to "getting ahead." For if we have a true present that is where everything happens.

Consulting the Runes is one way to "be here now." Working with them, you bypass the strictures of reason, the fetters of conditioning and the momentum of habit.* For the brief span of interacting with the Runes you are declaring a free zone in which your life is malleable, vulnerable, open to transformation. Just as the Vikings used the information provided by the Rune stones to navigate their ships under cloudy skies, so now you can use the Runes to modify your own life course. A shift of a few degrees at the beginning of your voyage will mean a vastly different position far out at sea.

Rune casting is high adventure. It means taking the wheel of your life and owning your power. The new maps, unlike the old, are three-dimensional, and the third dimension is Spirit. Whatever the Runes may be—intercessors for the self with the Self, simultaneous translators between the Self and the Divine, an ageless navigational aid—the energy that engages them is our own. And, ultimately, the wisdom as well. Thus, as we start to make contact with our deeps, we will begin to hear messages of profound beauty and true usefulness. For like snow-flakes and fingerprints, each of our oracular signatures is a one-of-a-kind aspect of Creation addressing its own.

*As Brugh Joy reminds us in his excellent book *Joy's Way: A Map for the Transitional Journey,* there are three sets of mental fetters to give up if you want to be truly free: judging, comparing and needing to know why. The "why" inevitably becomes clear as you progress in your passage.

THE RUNE OF HOSPITALITY

I saw a stranger yestereen;
I put food in the eating place,
   Drink in the drinking place,
   Music in the listening place;
And in the sacred names of the Triune
He blessed me and my house,
   My cattle and my dear ones.
And the lark said in her song:
   Often, often, often,
Goes the Christ in the stranger's guise:
   Often, often, often,
Goes the Christ in the stranger's guise.

From the Gaelic

Christ figure, Jaellinge, Sweden,
ca. A.D. 980

THE EMERGENCE
OF THE RUNES

A King he was on a carven throne
In many-pillared halls of stone
With golden roof and silver floor,
And runes of power upon the door.

J.R.R. Tolkien
The Fellowship of the Ring

Runes and charms are very practical formulae designed to produce
definite results, such as getting a cow out of a bog.

T. S. Eliot
The Music of Poetry

The wisdom of the Rune Masters died with them. Nothing remains but the sagas, the far-flung fragments of runic lore, and the Runes themselves.

In his fine book, *Runes: An Introduction*, Ralph W.V. Elliott writes of

strange symbols scratched into ancient tools and weapons now lying idle in some museum showcase; names of warriors, secret spells, even snatches of songs, appearing on objects as diverse as minute silver coins and towering stone crosses, scattered in the unlikeliest places from Yugoslavia to Orkney, from Greenland to Greece.*

The influence of the Runes on their time was incontestable. Elliott notes that when the high chieftains and wise counselors of Anglo-Saxon England met in conclave, they called their secret deliberations "runes," and that when Bishop Wulfila made his translation of the Bible into fourth-century Gothic, he rendered St. Mark's "the mystery of the kingdom of God" (Mark 4:11) using *runa* for "mystery." Eight centuries earlier, when Herodotus traveled around the Black Sea, he encountered descendants of Scythian tribesmen who crawled under blankets, smoked themselves into a stupor (a practice still met today in the Caucasus Mountains) and then cast sticks in the air and "read" them when they fell. Although these tribesmen were preliterate, their sticks would probably qualify as Runes.

There is no firm agreement among scholars as to where and when runic writing first made its appearance in Western Europe. Before the Germanic peoples possessed any form of script, they used pictorial symbols that they scratched into rocks. Especially common in Sweden, these prehistoric rock carvings or *hällristningar* are dated from the second Bronze Age (circa 1300 B.C.), and were probably linked to Indo-

*Ralph W. V. Elliott, *Runes: An Introduction* (Manchester, Eng.: Manchester University Press, 1959), p. 1.

European fertility and sun cults. The carvings include representations of men and animals, parts of the human body, weapon motifs, sun symbols, the swastika and variations on square and circular forms:

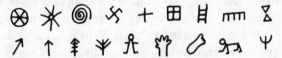

Elliott suggests an amalgamation of two separate traditions: "the alphabetic script on the one hand, the symbolic content on the other . . . The practice of sortilege (divination) was cultivated among Northern Italic as well as Germanic peoples, the one using letters, the others pictorial symbols."* Numerous *hällristningar,* as well as the runic standing stones, can still be seen in Germany and throughout Scandinavia today.

It is difficult for us to imagine the immense powers bestowed on the few who became skilled in the use of symbolic markings or glyphs to convey thought. Those first glyphs were called *runes,* from the Gothic *runa,* meaning "a secret thing, a mystery." The runic letter or *runastafr* became a repository for intuitions that were enriched according to the skill of the practitioner of *runemal,* the art of Rune casting.

From the beginning, the Runes took on a ritual function, serving for the casting of lots, for divination, and to evoke higher powers that could influ-

*Elliott, op. cit., pp. 64–5.

ence the lives and fortunes of the people. The craft of the Rune Masters and Mistresses touched every aspect of life, from the most sacred to the most practical. There were Runes and spells to influence the weather, the tides, crops, love, healing; Runes of fertility, cursing and removing curses, birth and death. Runes were carved on amulets, drinking cups, battle spears, over the lintels of dwellings and onto the prows of Viking ships.

The Rune Masters of the Teutons and Vikings wore startling garb that made them easily recognizable. Feared, honored, welcomed, these shamans were familiar figures in tribal circles. There is evidence that a fair number of runic practitioners were women. The anonymous author of the thirteenth-century *Saga of Erik the Red* provides a vivid description of a contemporary mistress of runecraft:

> She wore a cloak set with stones along the hem. Around her neck and covering her head she wore a hood lined with white catskins. In one hand she carried a staff with a knob on the end and at her belt, holding together her long dress, hung a charm pouch. She wore catskin shoes and catskin mittens to cover her hands at all times.

In pagan eyes, the earth and all created things were alive. Twigs and stones served for runic divination since, as natural objects, they embodied sacred powers. Runic symbols were carved into pieces of hardwood, incised on metal or cut into leather that was then stained with pigment into which human blood was sometimes mixed to enhance the potency of the spell. The most common Runes were smooth flat pebbles with symbols or glyphs painted on one side. The Rune Mistress would shake her pouch and scatter the pebbles onto the ground; those falling with glyphs upward were interpreted in answer to the question posed.

The most explicit surviving description of this procedure comes from the Roman historian Tacitus. Writing in A.D. 98 about practices prevalent among the Germanic tribes, he reports:

> To divination and casting of lots they pay attention beyond any other people. Their method of casting lots is a simple one: they cut a branch from a fruit-bearing tree and divide it into small pieces which they mark with certain distinctive signs *(notae)* and scatter at random onto a white cloth. Then, the priest of the community, if the lots are consulted publicly, or the father of the family, if it is done privately, after invoking the gods and with eyes raised to heaven, picks up three pieces, one at a time, and interprets them according to the signs previously marked upon them. (*Germania,* ch. X)

By Tacitus' time, the Runes were already becoming widely known on the continent—carried from place to place by traders, adventurers and warriors and, eventually, by Anglo-Saxon missionaries. For this to happen, a common alphabet was required—the alphabet that became known as *futhark* after its first six letters or glyphs:

f	u	th	a	r	k
ᚡ	ᚠ	ᚦ	ᚢ	ᚱ	ᚲ

Although later Anglo-Saxon alphabets expanded to include as many as thirty-three letters in Britain, the traditional Germanic futhark is comprised of twenty-four Runes. These were divided into three "families" of eight Runes, three and eight being numbers credited with magical potency. The three groups, known as *aettir,* were named for the Norse gods *Freyr, Hagal* and *Tyr.* The three *aettir* are:

Freyr's Eight: ᚡ ᚠ ᚦ ᚢ ᚱ ᚲ ᚷ ᚹ

Hagal's Eight: ᚺ ᚾ ᛁ ᛃ ᛇ ᛈ ᛉ ᛊ

Tyr's Eight: ᛏ ᛒ ᛖ ᛗ ᛚ ᛜ ᛟ ᛞ

It is with these twenty-four Runes, plus one later innovation, a Blank Rune, that *The Book of Runes* is concerned.

THE VIKING RUNES

When I began to work with the Runes, I had never seen a runic text, so I did not realize that I was breaking away from the traditional sequence of Freyr, Hagal and Tyr probably used by the early practitioners of *runemal*. But function determines form, use confers meaning and an Oracle always resonates to the requirements of the time in which it is consulted. I had to rely on the Runes themselves to establish their own order and to instruct me in their meanings.

The Rune stones I was working with had come to me in England: tiny brown rectangles hardly bigger than my thumbnail, with the glyphs scratched into the surfaces. The woman who made them lived on Trindles Road, in the Surrey town of Redhill. She hadn't glazed her Runes, merely baked them in her oven like cookies.

Along with this set of Runes came two Xeroxed sheets giving the glyphs, their approximate English meaning and a brief interpretation for each Rune when "Upright" or "Reversed." To the twenty-four futhark Runes had been added a Blank Rune represented simply as "The path of karma: that which is predestined and cannot be avoided. Matters hidden by the gods." There were no instructions for using the Runes and, after a few days, the Trindles Road Runes went onto a shelf.

But I kept the Runes and took them back to the States. Four years passed before I happened upon them again. I was alone on my Connecticut farm. It was a warm summer evening. I couldn't sleep, so I went to my study and began rearranging books. And there, in their little chamois bag, were the Runes.

I spilled them out onto my desk. As I moved the stones around, I got the same pleasurable feeling I had when I first handled them in England. It was then that it occurred to me to ask the Runes how they were to be employed. I sat quietly for a time, composing myself. I said a prayer, invoking the Holy Spirit, the Tao, my Higher Self, and all my Unseen Guides and Helpers. I opened my Oracle Journal, the notebook in which I record readings from the *I Ching*, and wrote out my question: "In what order do you wish to be arranged?" I noted the time, 10:55 P.M., and the date: June 21, the moment of the summer solstice.

I spread out the Runes, blank sides up, and moved them around, touching each Rune. Then, one by one, I turned them over, aligning them in front of me in three rows. It took only a few moments. When I was done, I sat and studied the arrangement:

I remember my first feeling was dismay that the Blank Rune, the Rune of karma, had not positioned itself more dramatically, rather than simply taking its place among the rest. And then I got an eerie feeling: the woman in England had said the Runes could be read *from right to left.* * Seen that way, the sequence began with what I now regard as the Rune of "The Self," and ended with the Blank Rune, the Rune that signals the presence of the Divine in our lives.

It was as I sat gazing at the Runes that these words came to me: *The starting point is the self. Its essence is water. Only clarity, willingness to change, is effective now. . . .* I moved to my typewriter and began to write. The Viking Runes had begun their teaching.

I worked on through the night, taking each Rune in my hand, just sitting with it, meditating on it, copying down what came to me. Now and then, when the flow dwindled, I turned to the *I Ching* and asked for a hexagram that revealed the essence of a particular Rune. The spirit of some of those readings is incorporated into the interpretations of the Viking Runes. By the time I had completed the interpretation of the Blank Rune, the sun was rising.

Since that long night, I have read a fair amount about the Runes and their history, the controversies over their origins, the speculations concerning their use. Only one thing is certain: beyond all the efforts of scholars to encompass them, the Runes remain elusive, for they are Odin's gift, and sacred.

Odin is the principal divinity in the pantheon of

*The Runes could face either way and be read from left or right or, on occasion, vertically. Some inscriptions even read *boustrophedon,* meaning in the manner in which a field is plowed. See illustration on page 33.

Norse gods. His name derives from the Old Norse for "wind" and "spirit," and it is through his passion, his transforming sacrifice of the self, that Odin brought us the Runes. Nine nights he hung on the *Yggdrasil,* the Tree of the World, wounded by his own blade, tormented by hunger, thirst and pain, unaided and alone until, before he fell, he spied the Runes and, with a last tremendous effort, seized them.

Next to the gift of fire, that of the alphabet is the great light in which we see our nature revealed. In *The Poetic Edda,* Odin, the great Rune Master, speaks across the centuries. Hear Odin now:

> *Do you know how to cut them, know how to*
> *stain them,*
> *Know how to read them, how to understand?*
> *Do you know how to evoke them, know how to*
> *send them,*
> *Know how to offer, know how to ask?*
>
> *It is better not to offer than to offer too much*
> *for a gift demands a gift,*
> *Better not to slay than to slay too many.*
> *Thus did Odin speak before the earth began*
> *when he rose up in after time.*
>
> *These runes I know, unknown to kings' wives*
> *Or any earthly man. "Help" one is called,*
> *For help is its gift, and helped you will be*
> *In sickness and care and sorrow.*

Another I know, which all will need
Who would study leechcraft.
On the bark scratch them, on the bole of trees
Whose bows bend to the east.

I know a third—
If my need be great in battle
It dulls the swords of deadly foes,
Neither wiles nor weapons wound me
And I go all unscathed . . .

So begins the sacred history of the Runes.

Boustrophedon script on stone
near Asferg, Sweden

I have no parents: I make the heavens and earth my parents.

I have no home: I make awareness my home.

I have no life or death: I make the tides of breathing my life and death.

I have no divine power: I make honesty my divine power.

I have no means: I make understanding my means.

I have no magic secrets: I make character my magic secret.

I have no body: I make endurance my body.

I have no eyes: I make the flash of lightning my eyes.

I have no ears: I make sensibility my ears.

I have no limbs: I make promptness my limbs.

I have no strategy: I make "unshadowed by thought" my strategy.

I have no designs: I make "seizing opportunity by the forelock" my design.

I have no miracles: I make right-action my miracles.

I have no principles: I make adaptability to all circumstances my principles.

I have no tactics: I make emptiness and fullness my tactics.

I have no talents: I make ready wit my talent.

I have no friends: I make my mind my friend.

I have no enemy: I make carelessness my enemy.

I have no armor: I make benevolence and righteousness my armor.

I have no castle: I make immovable-mind my castle.

I have no sword: I make absence of self my sword.

Annonymous Samurai, fourteenth century

3

CONSULTING
THE ORACLE

The real voyage of discovery consists not in seeking new landscapes but in having new eyes.

Marcel Proust

Lord, grant me weak eyes for things that are of no account and strong eyes for all thy truth.

Søren Kierkegaard

We walk by faith and not by sight.

St. Paul

Once you start exploring the world of Runes, you will discover that many people have developed their own form of personal Rune casting. I know a black man who works the boardwalk in Venice, California. He sits on an old sheet on which he has painted the rainbow circles of a bull's-eye. He has a bag of stones and shells and twigs, and when you have posed your question he scatters his Runes and reads from their spread. I have met people who work with sand dollars, bits of bone, stones upon which they have scratched their own symbols; I even know a woman who has discovered that the inside of the sea urchin's shell can be "read" effectively and employs a series of such shells for counseling. All of these variants, however homespun, seem to me consistent with the most ancient traditions such as the early Chinese practice of reading oracle bones and the cracks that appear in tortoiseshells heated in a fire, and with the tradition of *runemal* itself.

For the more conservative students of divination, there is what one of my friends calls "Noah Webster's Oracle." He merely opens the dictionary at random, taking his counsel from the words to which his finger points. At one moment while working intensively on this book, I was presented with several opportunities that I felt obliged to pass up; in doing so, I felt I was perhaps missing out, and I began giving myself a hard time. Instead of consulting the Runes on this issue, I opened a dictionary and, without looking, set my finger on the page. The counsel I received came under the words *lay off,* and contained (beneath my finger) the phrases "mark off boundaries . . . stop criticizing . . . minimize risk." I returned to my manuscript with a clear conscience.

Over the years, I have met a number of people who, without any precise knowledge of Oracles, employ the Bible in a similar fashion.*

---

*It has long been my habit to consult the *Daily Word* and to live by its wisdom. It is a teacher for me, a monthly book of daily Oracles.

While working with the Runes, I have considered what, at its most basic, constitutes a Rune. At what point is meaning present in a sign or glyph? Take a pen and paper. Fill the sheet with dashes, marks and signs in all the shapes you can imagine. Doing so soon becomes repetitive; there is only a limited number of marks you can make. Children write and carve all kinds of "runes," but they aren't producing Runes because children don't know what they are. Highway signs are a step up from this inchoate stage.

Have you noticed the Warrior Rune $\boxed{\rightarrow}$ on straightaways? Or the Rune of Opening Up $\boxed{\langle}$ $\boxed{\langle}$ in a series at certain curves? Meaning is clearly present, agreed upon, but hardly divinatory in nature—unless, of course, you happen to be mulling over an issue and see the sign at that moment, and it holds meaning for you.

I had a curious runic encounter in California while I was working on this book. One afternoon, driving out to the beach for a counseling session, I took the Las Virgenes–Malibu Canyon Road, a beautiful drive across the mountains. Coming out of a curve, I looked across the canyon and there, on the mountainside opposite, someone had painted a Rune the height of a man. No question about it—I was looking up at *Algiz* $\boxed{Y}$, the Rune of Protection. The glyph was painted on the rock face reversed, a call for caution in the runic vocabulary. The artist had enclosed the Rune in an oval so that it appeared like this: ⊛ . It took me a moment to realize that I was seeing a 1960s graffito from the antiwar movement. How strange that the movement had settled on a symbol of protection without ever knowing it. I drove on, wondering how runologists of the future would account for that isolated glyph. Centuries from now perhaps some graduate student will attempt to prove that the Vikings made it all the way to Malibu.

CONSULTING THE RUNES

No rules exist for consulting the Runes, beyond an attitude of seriousness and respect, for you are, in effect, consulting the Higher Self.

There are people who simply set aside a special time of day at which to cast the Runes. Others prefer a more ritual approach: lighting a candle, perhaps a stick of incense, taking time to compose themselves. A meditation on the breath is helpful. Simply follow the breath in and out; let the breaths be long, easy, connected. Become as still as you can manage, setting aside all considerations, worries, duties, if only for a moment; you can always get back to your current fears, regrets and anxieties later. Usually I try to say a brief prayer, even if the situation is intense or turbulent.

Focus is important. But if the ordinary business

of living intrudes, that's all right, too; the Runes are very forgiving. You can consult them on the run— no formal preparation, no sitting to still your mind. Your need is what brings the Runes into play. And always remember, you *are* in the realm of play, even if it is sacred play. The time to consult the Runes is when you have exhausted your own conscious wisdom, or when you are confronted with a situation where you seem to possess limited or incomplete information. If a crisis arises and you have cause to consult your Higher Self without delay, simply focus the issue clearly in your mind,* reach into the Rune bag, make contact with the stones, and draw a Rune. As one practitioner of *runemal* put it, "The right Rune always sticks to my fingers."

You can also consult the Runes for another person. If someone is far away and could benefit from the perspective of a Rune reading, the telephone is your ally. As a popular song says, "Telephone line is a lifeline." Many healers practice healing at a distance—time and space do not exist in spiritual healing. Rune reading works as well over 8,000 miles as it does face to face.

What kind of issues are appropriate?

An appropriate issue is *anything that relates to timeliness and right conduct.* You might wish counsel on a

---

*"Just as in interpreting a dream, one must follow the dream text with utmost exactitude, so in consulting the oracle, one must hold in mind the form of the question put, for this sets a definite limit to the interpretation of the answer." C. G. Jung, op. cit., p. xxxvi.

contemplated change in your way of life; on whether or not it is the proper moment to undertake a new livelihood, sell a business, make an investment, change your place of dwelling; on whether it is timely to terminate or undertake a relationship— these and similar concerns are the proper province for oracular interrogation.

Notice that I use the word *issues* rather than *questions.* For example, a question might be, "Should I end this relationship?" whereas to state it as an issue, you would say, "The issue is my relationship now." Instead of asking, "Should I accept this new job?" you might say "The issue is my work." This small distinction is a crucial one because by addressing the broader issue the Oracle allows the querent to extract the answer and take responsibility for the decision.

Whether I am consulting the Runes for others or for myself, they never fail to provide information that is relevant and to the point. When I am casting the Runes for others, I ask that they formulate the matter of concern clearly in their minds but *not* state it aloud. This eliminates any conscious personal bias in my interpretation of the Runes.

When you first start working with the Runes, you may want to check them for accuracy, in effect, to calibrate them. This can be done through *oracular cross talk:* consulting two different oracular instruments on the same issue. For years I have consulted the *I Ching.* When I began working with the Runes, in order to confirm their responses with those of a known and wise friend, I would address the same issue to the *I Ching* and then to the Runes. Time after time, I found both Oracles to be in resonance, sometimes identical in their symbolic content, often complementary, always an enrichment. My own confidence in the Runes was solidly confirmed through this process.

Occasionally, to my surprise and delight, the Oracle will go into *runic override,* answering in broader perspective than the issue posed. The Runes always seem clear as to what is truly at stake even when the querent is not. When the Runes employ their override in a matter, you are invariably put on notice that you are wanting in clarity and focus; that you have not, in fact, addressed the issue that most concerns you.

If you are ever in doubt about the timely issue to pose, simply ask the Runes: *What do I need to know in my life now?* The Oracle's reply is invariably nourishing and instructive.

Finally, there is a technique I have found most beneficial, and for which I am indebted to Dr. Allan W. Anderson. One of the techniques he suggests to the student of the *I Ching* is equally valid for the Runes. He calls it "The Rule of Right Action." Each morning consult the Oracle to determine your Rule of Right Action for the day. Make no mistake about it: you are not, by so doing, absolving yourself of responsibility for your own conduct. The reading you receive amounts to a psychic weather forecast, a configuration of atmospheric conditions for right conduct. Sometimes, when it has been a particularly trying or exhilarating day, you may again wish to consult the Oracle in the evening for an evaluation of how you've conducted yourself. If the idea of asking for a daily Rule seems excessive, try it on a weekly basis. Consult the Runes on Monday for the week's Rule, and again on Sunday night for your evaluation. Or take a monthly reading. It all depends on whether you prefer a close-up, medium- or long-range view of your passage.

As you establish your practice of consulting the Runes, you may find it profitable to log your issues and the guidance you receive. Since first beginning to work with the Runes, I have marked down the particular stones cast and a brief interpretation in my Oracle Journal; I also note the time, the date and, occasionally, the prevailing conditions in my life at the moment. Keeping such a journal allows you to observe the quality of your own progress as you work with the Oracle.

THE GREAT INVOCATION

From the point of Light within the mind of God
Let light stream forth into the minds of men.
Let Light descend on Earth.

From the point of Love within the Heart of God
Let Love stream forth into the hearts of men.
May Christ return to Earth.

From the center where the Will of God is known
Let purpose guide the little wills of men—
The purpose which the Masters know
and serve.

From the center which we call the race of men
Let the Plan of Love and Light work out
And may it seal the door where evil
dwells.

Let Light and Love and Power
Restore the Plan on Earth.

Alice Bailey

4

RUNEMAL: THE ART
OF RUNE CASTING

*Remember, you cannot abandon what you do not know. To go beyond
yourself, you must know yourself.*

Sri Nisargadatta Maharaj

Like all games, sacred and secular, the Runes are
meant to be "played" upon a field. The field represents the world that is always coming to be and
passing away. You may want to use a special piece
of fabric, colored or white, that you keep for this
purpose alone. When you unfold the cloth that
serves as your field, that very act can become a silent
meditation. My field, a rainbow weaving made for
me by a weaver of the Findhorn Community in Scot-
land, measures 14 inches by 18 inches and is woven
from twenty-two graded hues of silk thread.

My first bag was a found object: purple with a
legend stitched on one side announcing that the
bag's original contents had been a bottle of Crown
Royal whiskey. Someone else drank the whiskey; I
inherited the bag. I liked that bag because there was

plenty of room inside for even the largest hand to fit in and rattle the stones about. But neither bag nor field needs to be ornate; as the *I Ching* reminds us, "Even with slender means the sentiments of the heart can be expressed."

A Rune Master, in the ancient days, might shake the Runes in his pouch, chant an invocation to Odin, requesting that the god be present, and then scatter the stones, drawing his answer to the question for divination from those that fell glyph-side up. This venerable method seems unwieldy to me; when I employ it, I often find myself compelled to make a coherent interpretation from a dozen or more stones. However, a number of other satisfactory techniques recommend themselves.

In the beginning, whether I was reading for someone else or for myself, I used to spread all the Runes, glyphs down, on the field. Then I or the querent would touch each stone, moving it about or letting the fingers rest lightly upon it for a moment. But there is also something very satisfying about reaching into the bag and choosing the stones. I like feeling the stones click against one another and, even more, the way, after a few moments, a Rune seems always to insert itself between my fingers.

MAKING YOUR OWN RUNES

You may wish to make your own individual Runes, imbuing them with your energy, your vibrations. The material you select depends on your taste, artistic preferences and finances. I have cut Runes out of wood and branded the glyphs into them with a wood-burning set. A particularly lovely set of Runes was created for me by a Navajo silversmith for whom I had done a reading. Flat pebbles smoothed by the sea make beautiful Runes.

The first set of Runes I had made were of clay, twice glazed, by potter Norman Aufrichtig of Brookfield, Connecticut. When he fashioned and made the Viking Runes, he kept a daub of clay from the substance of each Rune and then formed the Blank Rune from those daubs; thus the Blank Rune contained symbolically the stuff of all life's elements.

If you make your own Runes, or make sets for others, let the doing be your meditation. The idea of meditating is a block for many people—including myself. I finally broke free from my anxiety about not being able to meditate conventionally when I heard Joseph Campbell say that underlining sentences in books was his meditation. Weeding in the garden can be a meditation. So can washing your car. And casting your Runes. The making is the first meditation.

Whether you create your own set of Runes or

acquire them, through touching and employing them with loving and respectful use you will make them yours.

TECHNIQUES AND SPREADS

There are a variety of methods for casting the Runes. Here are several techniques that I have found most effective.

Odin's Rune: This is the most practical and simple use of the Runes, and consists in drawing one Rune for an overview of an entire situation. That single Rune encompasses the issue, present conditions and resolution. In spirit, it is the nearest to the Delphic pronouncements of ancient times. This is the "crux" reading, the Rune of "Aha! So that's what it's all about."

Drawing Odin's Rune is also the technique for stressful conditions, for the use of the Spiritual Warrior under siege. You may find yourself in a pressure situation, confronted with matters that demand action now, and the truth is *you don't have enough information.* There is no time for spreading cloths, lighting candles, meditating. All you require is your bag of Runes and, if possible, a quiet place. I once had occasion to consult the Runes in a busy office where everyone was acting as if the world was coming to an end. The bathroom door was locked, so I got into the elevator and stopped it between floors. Those few moments between the seventh and eighth floors gave me privacy to compose myself. With the issue clearly in mind, I drew a single Rune and got *Fehu*, Nourishment and Possessions, which said, in effect: look at where your true nourishment lies.

I told this story to a friend who is a high corporate officer. When we met some months later, he informed me with a smile that he had been suddenly confronted with a supercritical situation that amounted to either taking over the company or resigning. "I headed for the men's room," he told me, "clutching my bag of Runes. When I came out, I was on my way to becoming the chief executive officer."

Nor is Odin's Rune valuable only in crisis conditions. The drawing of a single Rune is useful any time you want an overview of your situation. On a long drive or commute between home and work I almost always keep my Runes beside me on the seat. Drawing Odin's Rune has been a blessing to me time and again. Often, the Runes show me the humor in a heavy situation. And why not? God's favorite music is said to be laughter.

If you are worried about someone who is far away, before you rush to the telephone, focus on the person and draw a Rune. You will receive an instant "status report." This technique can be very consoling and very economical.

The printer who was making up my business cards showed interest in the runic symbols, and when I offered him the bag, he drew *Berkana* $\boxed{\text{B}}$, the Rune of Growth and Rebirth. Briefly, I gave him an interpretation. He replaced the Rune in the bag, started to move away, then turned back to me and said, "Wait, let me try something." He reached into the bag and drew again. He opened his hand and there was the same Rune. He grinned at me. It took me a moment to catch on—he was testing the Oracle! The Runes had passed the test, but I was left with an uncomfortable feeling.

The probability is that if you draw a Rune and then pose the same question an hour later, you will *not* receive the same Rune. The world has changed. Everything has changed.

The Three-Rune Spread: The magical number "three" figures prominently in the divination practices of the ancients and was, if we are to believe Tacitus, already in use 2,000 years ago. The Three-Rune Spread is quite satisfying for all but the most extended and intricate readings. (As of this writing, I have done almost 600 castings, relying upon this spread more than half the time.) With the issue clearly in mind, select three Runes, one at a time, and place them in order of selection *from right to left* on the field.* To avoid the risk of manipulating the stones, especially as you become familiar with their sym-

---

*If you prefer, you can place the Runes vertically from top to bottom and read them in order of selection.

bols, it is preferable to place them with their blank sides up; only nine Runes read the same Upright or Reversed; with the other sixteen, the readings will differ with the position of their glyphs. It is to be hoped that, even with regular use, your stones will not pick up identifying marks on their blank faces.

Once you have selected the Runes, they will lie before you in this fashion:

Depending on how you happen to turn them, you may now still alter the direction of the glyphs, but that, too, is part of the process.

Now let us consider an example of a Three-Rune Spread. One of my friends, whose wife had recently left him, was still in primary shock when he came to me for a Rune casting. He was experiencing a lot of pain, realizing, after the fact, the value of this relationship and agonizing over his loss. The issue, then, was "What am I to learn from this separation?"

These are the Runes he drew:

Interpreting the Runes may be done in the following manner: the first Rune (on the right) ᛉ speaks to the situation as it is; the second Rune (center) ᚲ suggests the course of action called for; and the third Rune (on the left) ᚾ indicates the new situation that is evolving. Reading from the right, the first Rune, *Algiz* ᛉ , the Rune of Protection Reversed, addresses his sense of being totally vulnerable, unprotected. It is a counsel to be mindful that only right action and correct conduct provide protection at such a time. Don't try to protect yourself; you will progress, and that knowledge is your protection. You must learn and grow from what has happened. . . . The second Rune, *Kano* ᚲ , is the Rune of Opening Up. Trust the process, this Rune is saying; you now have more light with which to see what is the case, what in your old conditioning must go. . . . Third comes *Nauthiz* ᚾ , the Rune of Constraint and Pain (a Rune frequently drawn these days, it seems). The growth to be undertaken will not be free of anguish. His wife's departure from his life has enabled him to undertake serious work on himself, and he is put on notice that rectification must come before progress.

To sum up, the three Runes were saying: though you are vulnerable and exposed, with the pain comes the necessary clarity to get on with self-change; and as you progress, remember to consider the positive uses of adversity. Despite the Reversed Rune and the pain involved, I felt—and so did he—that this was a positive and encouraging reading.

There is another useful method of interpreting the Three-Rune Spread, particularly when the issue is one of blockage in your life. In this interpretation, the Rune you draw first represents *You Now*, where you are in your passage. The third Rune, on the left, stands for the *Goal* you wish to attain, while the second or center Rune is the *Problem*, whatever is blocking you from reaching your goal. So from right to left the Runes are:

If you decide upon this method of interpretation, do so in advance. In most cases, the Runes drawn will not be identical with those you get from employing the "three stages" reading of *situation as it is, course of action called for, new situation evolving*, demonstrated above.

The conclusion of a Rune casting occurs not when you have completed your interpretation of a spread, but when the stones are returned to their bag by the person who drew them.

The Runic Cross: Employ this spread when you want a more complete picture of any situation and its dynamics. This spread, inspired by the Tarot, calls for selecting six Runes, which are laid out in the form of a Runic or Celtic Cross. The pattern is as follows:

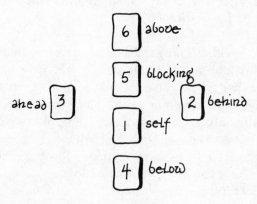

The first Rune represents the *self,* you now; the second, the *Behind* Rune, is that from which you are coming, what lies directly behind you; the third, the *Ahead* Rune, stands for what lies ahead of you, what is coming into being; the *Below* Rune represents the foundation of the matter under consideration, the unconscious elements and forces involved; the fifth or *Blocking* Rune tells you the nature of the obstacles between you; the sixth or *Above* Rune indicates the best outcome you can anticipate.

A considerable amount of information is housed in the Runic Cross, and this spread is always a source of long thoughts. If after laying out and considering these six Runes you still lack clarity, replace all the Runes in their bag and draw a single Rune. This seventh Rune will give you the crux or gist of the situation; it is what my friend Hilda Brown calls "the Rune of Resolution."

Rune Poker: This game can be played with utmost pleasure and profit by two people who truly care for each other. It can also be played with your worst enemy, and with equal profit. Since the Runes make available information from our deeps, places we cannot always reach directly and whose truths we are hard pressed to express unaided, Rune Poker is a potent tool for interpersonal dialogue.

Each player should have a set of Runes. Select three Runes from your bag, and place them in front of you, glyph-side down. Then play one. Each of you turns one Rune over. Your Rune becomes your statement to the other. Winning is not really at issue here. Rather, this technique ritualizes what conversation really is about: with no rules that restrict, the focus is on what people want/need to discuss, and play that lasts as long as seems suitable. You may want to employ more Runes, exhausting the possibilities of each before laying down the next. At the conclusion of play, summarize the essence of the Runes played.

At first, try Rune Poker two-handed. Say you are playing with a lover at a time when some unclarity has crept into the relationship. She plays *Laguz,* the Rune of Water, Flow, That Which Conducts Reversed $\lrcorner$ —a statement to the man to get in touch with his own true feminine if he hopes to understand her. His play is *Raido,* the Rune of Journey, Communication, Union and Reunion $\mathbb{R}$, a statement of his willingness to keep on removing resistances, regulating excesses. On the second round, he plays *Uruz,* the Rune of Strength, Manhood $\sqcap$, an indication that he is undergoing a transition, claiming back a part of himself, a part he has been living out through another, possibly her. Her play is *Hagalaz,* the Rune of Disruptive Natural Forces, Elemental Power H , indicating an urge for freedom, a warning that she is waking up to herself, and will, if necessary, sacrifice security and relationships in order to grow. . . . Watching the hand develop is most revealing although not, on every occasion, free of discomfort. But then, true growth rarely is.

Rune Poker can also be played by a close-knit group of colleagues or associates working on a project. Say you are doing research and development on a new invention, and the process is blocked. Three or four of you may want to declare a poker break. Each Rune dealt becomes a statement of the player's position, attitude or problem. I make my statement, you respond. The three-Rune progression can also be: You-Rune, Blockage-Rune, Best Outcome-Rune. The game swiftly takes on strategic and therapeutic overtones. Everyone will learn as much as they can handle, and there will be no lack of humor along the way.

The applications of Rune Poker are numerous. You will find that as you play it you develop variations and new procedures of your own.

Three-Lifetimes Spread: * This spread is for those who regard reincarnation as a viable possibility. It furnishes a three-level perspective on your passage, and is laid out on the Rune of Fertility, *Inguz* $\boxed{\text{X}}$. The Runes represent (in order of casting): 1) Birth and Childhood Conditions, 2) Your Present Situation, 3) Future in This Life, 4) Past Incarnation and 5) Future Incarnation. The Runes are laid out in this manner:

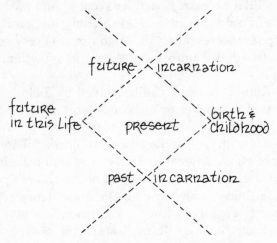

*Lifetimes are not necessarily sequential. The lifetime closest to you *karmically*, the lifetime influencing your passage now, may not be the last one lived. While time as we perceive it is a linear experience, such is not necessarily the case in Eternity.

The first reading I undertook with this Three-Lifetimes Spread was on my own account. This was the outcome:

Birth and Childhood Conditions inform me that I came into this life needing to learn to relate rightly to Constraint and Pain ⊬ ; that I must learn to work with the "shadow" areas in myself, the areas of stunted growth, weaknesses I project negatively onto others. I was put on notice that I could expect holdups and setbacks until I had rectified the imbalances in my nature. My *Present Situation* is signified by the Rune of Beneficial Outcomes ⟨⟩ , a span of time leading to Harvest, during which I must exercise patience and cultivate my nature with care. My *Future in This Life* is represented by the Rune of Wholeness, Life Force ϟ , the impulse toward self-realization and regeneration, the recognition of something long denied, and the attendant warning not to give myself airs. The Rune of Transformation ⋈ stands in the *Past Incarnation* position, indicating a major breakthrough to be the ground from which this present passage springs; a tremendously positive Rune with assured outcome and radical growth as its features, it indicates that I had done considerable hard work that time around. And finally, the *Future Incarnation* is represented by the Rune of Avertive Powers and Defenses ⎡↑⎤ , an indication that the power I am funding in this passage, the tests I am undergoing, will enable me to avoid blockage and to continue my growth in the upcoming incarnation.

Since it is a destiny profile, the Three-Lifetimes Spread should not be undertaken lightly or in a state of agitation. This casting provides you with information about what you still need to deal with from your past so that you can change your present situation, thus affecting both your future in this life and your next incarnation.

You may find this spread helpful in evaluating your relationships with people who are close to you, with potential business partners and even for better understanding the motives and behavior of our national leaders.

Essentially, the Three-Lifetimes Spread is an evolving runic horoscope. As you change and evolve, it changes and evolves, providing you with a real-time map of your progress in the spiritual life.

Two Cautions: Before you cast the Runes for another person who is not present, it is only basic courtesy to ask whether such action is timely and correct. Ask for a "Yes" or a "No" by the most direct method: simply reach into your bag and draw a Rune. Upright is Yes, Reversed, No. If you happen to draw one of the nine Runes that read the same Upright and Reversed, draw again. There may be times when you should not consult the Runes on your own behalf, but rather go by your gut feeling. When in doubt, ask. Many issues can be resolved with common sense and an open heart.

Finally, *do not lend your Runes to others.* They are for your personal use. Your prayers, your yearning for more Light, your perseverance in self-change will inform and infill them. Some people find that they are not even comfortable consulting the Runes for others. Remember that the energy invested in your Runes is your energy; it is a personal blessing bestowed on the self by the Self.

As you become familiar with your Runes, you will no doubt discover new and creative ways to utilize them. I recently heard from a woman, a painter, whose approach to life is preeminently visual. "I lay out the stones," she wrote, "and look at them. I meditate on each one. One is always stronger than the rest. The shape picks for me." I would be grateful to hear from you about your own experiences and the way you work with the Runes.

The Viking Runes, ancient as they are, remain an open-ended system with a future probably longer than its past.

5

THEATER
OF THE SELF

*We are all teachers, and what we teach is what we need to learn, and
so we teach it over and over again until we learn it.*

A principle of *A Course in Miracles*

Almost five months after the summer solstice
brought me their order and meanings, the Runes
communicated with me once again.

I was driving south along the Pacific Coast
Highway when, suddenly, I got a strong feeling
about the interrelated sequence of the Runes. I understood that each Rune was linked to the next not
merely by meaning, but through a progressive development from Rune to Rune and carrying through the
entire runic alphabet. The alphabet, in effect, dis-
played the twenty-five steps of the self growing into
wholeness.

Without bothering to pull off the road, I opened
my Rune notes and, starting with the first letter,
jotted down the essential meaning for each Rune,

connecting it to its neighbor. I wrote steadily as I drove, still in the fast lane, using the steering wheel as my table and glancing between the page and the highway. The miles passed by and all the connections flowed into place. I was just coming to the Blank Rune when I caught a movement out of my right eye. Beyond the car window and staring at me with an expression that said "I don't believe this!" was a California highway patrolman on his motorcycle. My speedometer registered 72 mph. We both pulled over. I didn't even try to explain.

At the roadside, I completed the Blank Rune. When I got home I copied what I had written, observing its pattern, listening to its rhythm. Not only did the progression hold, it fell into five balanced clusters or acts. Here then are the Viking Runes, divided into Five Acts, in the play of the self coming to the Self.

Act I: The starting point is the self ᛗ that, in its willingness to change, undertakes Partnership ᚷ at the highest level—Partnership with the Divine—and in so doing receives the Gift of freedom. The self is enabled in its work by the Messenger Rune ᚨ , which operates between the Divine and the self through Signals in the form of new connections, the linkages of self-change. During this process, there occurs a peeling away, bringing Separation and Retreat ᛟ and loosing the bonds we have inherited from being in the world. Once this transformation is underway, the Strength becomes available ble for growth into Manhood and Womanhood $\boxed{\text{ᚢ}}$.

Act II: This is the moment of Initiation $\boxed{\text{ᚲ}}$ that leads to new wholeness; the process occurs at an inner level and nothing external matters here. Now the self undergoes the Pain of Necessary Constraint $\boxed{\text{ᚾ}}$ in order to be cleansed and healed, for rectification precedes progress. Out of the cleansing comes Fertility, New Beginnings $\boxed{\text{ᛜ}}$. Since the new creature is totally vulnerable, Defense is provided, Avertive Powers $\boxed{\text{ᛇ}}$, to ward off injury, and, akin to these, another more positive form of Protection $\boxed{\text{ᛉ}}$, which calls for correct conduct and timely action; to progress well is the best protection.

Act III: Now the self can receive the Nourishment $\boxed{\text{ᚠ}}$ it requires, either in the form of Possessions or through well-being and self-rule. This brings Joy and Happiness from within $\boxed{\text{ᚹ}}$, a sense of having come to oneself. There follows next a period of waiting for the Harvest $\boxed{\text{ᛃ}}$, a time marked by patience and perseverance and careful cultivation until, at the harvest time, the self experiences an Opening Up $\boxed{\text{ᚲ}}$, new Light in which both to receive and to know the joy of giving. And by this new Light is revealed the birth of the Spiritual Warrior $\boxed{\text{ᛏ}}$, who possesses the power of discrimination by which to cut away the old outgrown life. With the birth of the Spiritual Warrior, we arrive at the Third Act curtain.

Act IV: As the Spiritual Warrior pursues the path with a heart, Growth ᛒ is the concern, the flowing of things into new forms. There is no urge to turn back. The self is more centered, better prepared when, with Movement ᛗ , changes and progress come; for as we cultivate our nature, all else follows. There is increased attunement with the feminine, Fluidity, That Which Conducts ᛚ , and at this level another cleansing and balancing occur. Now we are prepared for the upsurge of Natural Forces That Disrupt us totally ᚺ as old dead ways of being fall away. At last, a new synthesis is possible, marked by Communication and a journey of Reunion ᚱ with the Higher Self on the path to Union with the Divine.

Act V: The path reaches upward, climbing to a final peak, a Gateway ᚦ where Non-Action is called for, and meditation on the progress so far. Integration is the hallmark of this second stage of Initiation. For beyond the Gateway lies a major Breakthrough, a Transformation ᛞ signified by the leap of Faith. Then everything is blocked, the way Impeded ᛁ until, out of that icebound stage the Sun, Life Force ᛋ liberates new energies, a new way of being. And finally, the Spiritual Warrior arrives at the Rune of All-in-All, the Blank Rune

☐ , from whose blankness comes again, in eternal renewal, the starting point for the self. . . .

At the end of Act V, you are once more at the beginning. As you undergo your passage, there are twelve Runes that focus directly upon the mechanism of self-change. The Twelve, taken together, comprise a *Cycle of Self-Transformation.* These Runes are nodal points along the path of self-change and, in themselves, make up an energy framework within the body of the runic alphabet; an armature, so to speak, sustaining and facilitating the process of transformation. The Twelve are: (3) Signals, Messenger Rune, The God Loki; (4) Separation, Retreat, Inheritance; (5) Strength, Manhood, Womahood, A Wild Ox; (6) Initiation, Something Hidden, A Secret Matter; (7) Constraint, Necessity, Pain; (8) Fertility, New Beginnings, The Hero-God Ing; (16) Growth, Rebirth, A Birch Tree; (17) Movement, Progress, A Horse; (19) Disruptive Natural Forces, Elemental Power, Hail; (20) A Journey, Communication, Union, Reunion; (21) Gateway, Place of Non-Action; (22) Breakthrough, Transformation, Day. When two or more of the Twelve are conjoint in a spread, the potential for growth and integration is greatly enhanced.

6

INTERPRETING
THE RUNES

The seed of God is in us. Pear seeds grow into pear trees, nut seeds into nut trees, and God seeds into God.

Meister Eckhart

The final part of this book is the only part you really need—that and your set of Rune stones. I am passing on this gift to you in the sure hope that it will enrich your life as it has mine.

The Runes found me. And they found me quite ignorant of their history and use. Eventually I understood: it is as well that an introductory handbook such as this one be written by someone who is feeling his way, just as readers of this book, encountering the power of the Runes for the first time, must feel their way. For with the Runes we are in the presence of the numinous, the Divine. Scholarship is not necessary. Only the listening heart is necessary.

In approaching an ancient mystery a surrender is required. The poet Robert Bly said, "There are hundreds of ways to kneel and kiss the ground." An image recurs from time to time in my mind. I see a vast misty field containing some Stonehenge that did not survive. It lies within view of a glacier, this field, high above the mouth of a wild fjord. As I watch, out of the mists emerge the great stones; looming overhead they constellate at their stations, massive, weathered, blossoming with yellow lichen. There is something military about the way they stand in ranks to form a square. At the same time, a powerful sense of the sacred invests the scene. Above the rustle of eelgrass, the deeply carved glyph in each stone seems to pulse and vibrate. These stones are the markers left by Spiritual Warriors, the servants of civilization. This is the computer they built for us. And at the square's very center, touched by the sun's first rays, stands a blank and solitary stone: *both pregnant and empty, arbiter of all that is coming to be and passing away.* . . .

The praying voices of the Old Ones are silent. Three hundred years have passed. No doubt those voices have whispered to others as they whispered to me. We must be content with whispers, honor our own natures and trust the Knowing Self within.

The Runes are a major blessing, a gift from the Knowing Self that is our beginning and our destination. A talisman for our journey and a tool for self-counseling, the Runes speak to each of us according to our ability to hear. As available as we are accessible, truly democratic, they are an agency of the process by which we grow in clarity, in stillness, in being at one with the Self. To that end one single question, a simple prayer, will always suffice: *Show me what I need to know for my life now.*

What follows is what the Runes taught me about themselves.

The Self

Mannaz

The starting point is the self. Its essence is water. Only clarity, willingness to change, is effective now. A correct relationship to your self is primary, for from it flow all possible correct relationships with others and with the Divine.

Remain modest—that is the Oracle's counsel. Regardless of how great may be your merit, be yielding and devoted, moderate and correct, for then you have a true direction for your way of life.

Be in the world but not of it. That is implicit here. And yet do not be closed, or narrow, or judging. Remain receptive to impulses flowing from the Divine within and without. Here you might contemplate the words from *Hamlet:* "To thine own self be true." And these words, too, may be contemplated: *strive to live the ordinary life in a non-ordinary way.* Remember at all times what is coming to be and passing away, and focus on that which abides. Nothing less is called for from you now. This is a time of major growth and rectification; and as a rule rectification must come before progress.

This is not a time for trying to get "credit" for accomplishments, but rather seek to fulfill the time span, content to do your task for the task's sake, which is the meaning of "immanent activity." This is more a problem for those whose eyes are always on the goal than it is for those who have not forgotten how to play and can more easily and readily lose themselves in doing the work for its own sake. Herein lies the secret of experiencing a *true present*.

If you take the Rune of the Self and cut it down the middle, you get the Rune for Joy with its mirror image. There is a subtle caution here against carelessness. The dancing acrobatic energy of balancing is called for now—the Self is required to balance the self. *Nothing in excess* was the second phrase written over the gateway to the temple at Delphi. The first counsel was *Know thyself.* With these words, the alphabet of the Viking Runes begins.

Reversed: If you feel you are blocked, this Rune urges you to begin by being clear with yourself— facing up, admitting, releasing, whatever it takes. Do not turn to others now, but look inside, in silence, for the enemy of your progress. No matter what area of your life seems to you to be blocked or thwarted, stop and reconsider: you will recognize the outer "enemy" as but a reflection of what you have not, before now, been willing or able to recognize as coming from within.

Above all do not give yourself airs. The momentum of past habits is the challenge here: in the life of the Spirit you are always at the beginning.

Partnership
A Gift

Gebo

Drawing this Rune is an indication that union, uniting or partnership in some form is at hand. But you are put on notice not to collapse yourself into that union. For true partnership can only be achieved by separate and whole beings who retain their separateness even in unity and uniting. Remember to let the winds of Heaven dance between you.

At all levels—in love relationships, in business matters, in partnering of every kind—this counsel applies particularly when you enter into partnership with the Higher Self. Establishing an open, flowing channel between the self and the Self is the ultimate form of human partnership. For out of it comes union with the Divine; God always enters into equal partnerships.

Thus *Gebo,* the Rune of Partnership, has no Reverse for it signifies the gift of freedom from which flow all other gifts.

Signals
Messenger Rune
The God Loki

Ansuz

This is the first of the twelve Runes that make up the Cycle of Self-Transformation, Runes that focus directly upon the mechanism of self-change. The keynote here is *receiving:* messages, signals, gifts. Even a timely warning may be seen as a gift. When the Messenger Rune brings sacred knowledge, one is truly blessed.

The message may be that of a new life unfolding. New lives begin with new connections, surprising linkages that direct us into new pathways. Take pains to be especially aware and conscious during meetings, visits, chance encounters, particularly with persons wiser than yourself. A sense of new family solidarity invests *Ansuz.*

Through association with the Norse god Loki, Mercury overshadows this Rune. In mythology a strange, androgynous figure, keeper of the keys to knowledge, Mercury carried messages between the gods and between gods and humanity. In him is symbolized the urge to integrate unconscious motive with conscious recognition. Drawing this Rune tells you: connection with the Divine is at hand.

This Rune is a signal to explore the depths, the foundations of life, and to experience the inexhaustible wellspring of the Divine in your nature. You are reminded that you must draw first from the well to nourish and give to yourself. Then there will be more than enough to nourish others.

Reversed: You may well be concerned over what appears to be failed communication, lack of clarity or awareness either in your past history or in a present situation. Equally, you may feel concern because of difficulties that inhibit you from accepting what is offered. Then again a sense of futility, of wasted motion, of a fruitless journey may dismay you. Remember, however, that this is one of the Cycle Runes. What is happening is timely in your process. If the well is clogged, this is the moment for cleaning out the old. Reversed, this Rune is saying, "Consider the uses of adversity."

4

Othila

Retreat
Separation
Inheritance

Real property is associated with this Rune, for *Othila* is the Rune of acquisition and benefits. It seems strange to say, but the benefits you receive, the "inheritance," may be derived from something you must give up. This can be particularly difficult when that which you are called upon to give up or abandon is part of your background, your cultural inheritance. For then you must look closely at what, until now, you have proudly claimed as your birthright. Whether it is your attachment to your position in society, to the work you do or even to your beliefs about your own nature, the separation called for now will free you to become more truly who you are.

This is a time of separating paths. Old skins must be shed, outmoded relationships discarded. When this Rune appears in a spread, a peeling away is called for. This is a Rune of radical severance.

The proper action here is submission and, quite probably, retreat. Retreat in the sense of reserve in your conduct; of knowing how and when to retreat and possessing the firmness of will to carry it out.

Reversed: The warning is that you take pains not to be mechanical or unaware. This is not a time to be bound by old conditioning, old authority. Ask yourself what feels right for you and act according to the Light you possess now in your life. Because you may be called upon to undertake a radical departure from old ways, total honesty is required. Otherwise, through negligence or refusal to see clearly, you may cause pain to others, damage to yourself.

Not rigidity but flow is the proper attitude at this time. And yet you must wait for the universe to act. Drawing this Rune remember: we do without doing, and everything gets done.

5

Strength
Manhood, Womanhood

Uruz　　　　　　　# A Wild Ox

The Rune of termination and new beginnings. Drawing it indicates that the life you have been living has outgrown its form, which must die so that life energy can be released in a new birth, a new form. *Uruz* is a Rune of passage and, as such, part of the Cycle of Self-Transformation.

Positive growth and change, however, may involve passage into darkness as part of the cycle of perpetual renewal. As in Nature, the progression consists of five parts: death, decay, gestation, germination, rebirth. Events occurring now may well prompt you to undergo a death within yourself. Since self-change is never coerced—we are always free to resist—remain mindful that the new form, the new life, is always greater than the old.

Prepare, then, for opportunity disguised as loss. It could involve the loss of someone or something to which there is an intense emotional bond, and *through* which you are living a part of your life, a part that must now be retrieved so you can live it out for yourself. Now, in some way, that bond is being severed, a relationship radically changed, a death experienced. Seek among the ashes and discover a new perspective and a new birth.

The original meaning of this symbol was "a wild ox" (the aurochs). When the wild ox was domesticated—a nearly impossible task—it could transport heavy loads. Learn to adapt yourself to the demands of such a creative time. Firm principles attach to this Rune, and at the same time humility is called for since in order to rule you must learn how to serve. This Rune puts you on notice that your soul and the universe support the new growth.

Reversed: Without ears to hear and eyes to see, you may fail to take advantage of the moment. The negative result could well be an opportunity missed, the weakening of your position. It may seem that your own strength is being used against you.

For some, this Rune Reversed will serve to alert, providing clues in the form of minor failures and disappointments. For others, those more deeply unconscious or unaware, it should provide a hard jolt. Reversed, it calls for some serious thoughts about the quality of your relationship to your Self.

But take heart. Remember the constant cycling of death and rebirth, the endless going and return. Everything we experience has a beginning, a middle, and end, and is followed by a new beginning. Therefore do not draw back from the passage into darkness. When in deep water, become a diver.

6

Initiation

Something Hidden

Perth   A Secret Matter

A hieratic or mystery Rune pointing to that which is beyond our frail manipulative powers. This Rune is on the side of Heaven, the Unknowable, and has associations with the phoenix, that mystical bird that consumes itself in the fire and then rises from its own ashes. Its ways are secret and hidden.

Deep inner transformational forces are at work here. Yet what is achieved is not easily or readily shared. An integrity is involved that may be masked, disguised or secret. After all, becoming whole, the means of it, is a profound secret.

On the side of the earthly or mundane, there may well be surprises; unexpected gains are not un-likely. On the side of human nature, this Rune is symbolized by the flight of the eagle. Soaring flight, free from entanglement, lifting yourself above the endless ebb and flow of ordinary life to acquire broader vision—all this is indicated here. This is the Rune of question.

Another of the Cycle Runes, *Perth* signifies an intense aspect of initiation. *Nothing external matters here,* except as it shows you its inner reflection. This Rune is concerned with the deepest stratum of being, with the bedrock on which your fate is founded. For some, *Perth* means experiencing a psychic death. If need be, let go of everything, no exceptions, no exclusions. Nothing less than renewal of the Spirit is at stake.

Reversed: A counsel against expecting too much, or expecting in the ordinary way, for the old way has come to an end; you simply cannot repeat the old and not suffer. Reversed, this Rune puts you on notice to call in your scattered energies and concentrate on your own life at this moment, your own requirements for growth. More important, this Rune counsels you not to focus on outcomes, or to bind yourself with the memory of past achievements; in so doing, you rob yourself of a *true present,* which is the only time in which self-change can be realized.

You may feel overwhelmed with exhaustion from meeting obstruction upon obstruction in your passage. Yet you always have a choice, you can see all this apparent negativity as "bad luck" or you can recognize it as an obstacle course, a challenge peculiar to the initiation you are presently undergoing. Then each setback, each humiliation becomes a test of character. When your inner being is shifting and reforming on a deep level, patience, constancy and perseverance are called for. So stay centered, see the humor, and keep on keeping on.

7

Constraint
Necessity
Pain

Nauthiz

Upright or Reversed, this is a difficult Rune. The necessity of relating to severe constraint is its lesson. Its positive aspects represent the limitations we directly cause ourselves; its negative side attracts limitations from people around us. Both are equally difficult to handle. The role of *Nauthiz* is to identify our "shadow" areas, places where growth was stunted, resulting in weaknesses we project negatively onto others. Try not to take this world personally, this Rune is saying, work with the shadow, examine what inside you magnetizes misfortune into your life. When you are able to look upon this Rune with a smile, you will recognize the troubles, denials and setbacks of life as your guides, teachers and developers.

The need for restraint is unquestionable here. Drawing this Rune puts you on notice that there will be holdups, reasons to consider your plans carefully. Only remember: your dissatisfactions are not unreasonable, because there *is* work to be done on your self. So take it on with good will and show perseverance.

This is a time to pay off old debts, to restore, if not harmony, at least balance. So mend, restore, redress. When fishermen can't go to sea they repair nets. Let the constraints of the time serve you in righting your relationship to your Self. Be mindful that rectification comes before progress. And once again, consider the uses of adversity.

Reversed: When something within us is disowned, that which is disowned wreaks havoc. A cleansing is required here; in undertaking it you fund a will and strengthen character. Begin with what is most difficult and proceed to what is easy. Remember that "suffering," in its original sense, merely meant "undergoing." Thus you are required to undergo the dark side of your passage. To control your anger, to restrain your instincts, to keep your faith firm—all this is at issue here. Modesty and good temper are the essential blessings at such a time.

As part of the Cycle of Self-Transformation, *Nauthiz* is the great teacher disguised as the bringer of pain and limitation. It has been said that only at the point of greatest darkness do we become aware of the Light within us by which we come to recognize the true creative power of the Self.

8

Inguz

Fertility
New Beginnings
The Hero–God Ing

This Rune is akin to the moon, to the yin, the intuitive energy with its urge toward harmonizing and adjusting in the sphere of personal relationships. It embodies the need to share, the yearning to be desired, a search after similarities.

The completion of beginnings is what *Inguz* requires. It may mark a time of joyous deliverance, of new life, a new path. A Rune of great power, it indicates that the force is available to achieve completion, resolution, from which comes a new beginning. Above all, completion is crucial here. It may be timely that you complete a project now; if so, make that your first priority. Perhaps a difficult state of mind can be resolved, clarified, turned around. The appearance of this Rune in a spread indicates that you must fertilize the ground for your own deliverance.

All things change, and we cannot live permanently amid obstructions. With deliverance comes the release from tensions and uncertainty. As you resolve and clear away the old, you will experience a release. The period at or just prior to birth is often a dangerous one. Now it is time to enter the delivery room. Movement involves danger, and yet movement that is timely leads out of danger. This Rune signals your emergence from a closed, chrysalis state. Prior to "breaking out" you may be required to free yourself from a rut, habit or relationship; to free yourself from some deep cultural pattern, some activity that was quite proper to the self you are leaving behind.

Another of the Cycle Runes, *Inguz* counsels preparation. Being centered and grounded, your space cleared of all unwanted influences, and seeing the humor, you are indeed prepared to open to the Will of Heaven, and can await your deliverance with calm certainty.

9

Eihwaz

Defense
Avertive Powers
Yew Tree

As we are tested we fund the power to avert blockage and defeat. At the same time, we develop in ourselves an aversion to the conduct that brings us into stressful situations.

There appears to be blockage in your path, but even a delay may prove beneficial. Do not be overly eager to press forward. This is not a time or situation in which you can make your influence felt. Patience is the counsel *Eihwaz* offers. Nothing hectic, no acting needy or lusting after a desired outcome. This Rune speaks to the difficulties that arise at the beginning of new life. Often it announces a time of waiting: for a spring to fill up with water, for fruit to ripen on the bough.

Perseverance and foresight are called for here. The ability to foresee consequences before you act is the mark of the profound person. Avert anticipated difficulties through right action. We are not *doers*, but we are *deciders*. Once our decision is clear, the doing becomes effortless, for then the universe supports and empowers our action.

Receiving the Rune *Eihwaz* you are put on notice that through inconvenience and discomfort, growth is promoted. This may well be a trying time; certainly it is a meaningful one. Set your house in order, tend to business, be clear and wait on the Tao, the Will of Heaven.

10

Algiz

Protection
Sedge or Rushes
An Elk

Control of the emotions is at issue here. In transit and transition, shifts in life course and accelerated self-change, it is important not to collapse yourself into your emotions—the highs as well as the lows. This time offers ample mental exercise and stimulation. New opportunities and challenges are typical of this Rune. And with them will come trespasses and unwanted influences.

Algiz serves as a mirror for the Spiritual Warrior, the one whose battle is always with the self. The protection of the Warrior is like the curved horns of the elk, or like the sedge grass, for both serve to keep open space around you. Remain mindful that timely action and correct conduct are the only true protection. If you find yourself feeling pain, observe the pain, stay with it. Don't try to protect yourself from life or pull the veil down and escape by denying what is happening. You *will* progress; knowing that is your protection.

Reversed: Look carefully at all associations you form at this time. Be thoughtful about your health and alert not to add weight to the burdens others are carrying. If you see fit to become involved with people who are "using" you, stay conscious of that fact and take responsibility for your own position; then you can only benefit. And yet regardless of whether your enterprise prospers or suffers, do not be concerned: you may not win, but you will never lose, for you will always learn from what takes place. Temperance and courtesy are the sinews of this Rune's protective powers.

II

Fehu

Possessions
Nourishment
Cattle

This is a Rune of fulfillment: ambition satisfied, rewards received, love fulfilled. It also promises nourishment, from the most worldly to the sacred and Divine. For if the ancient principle "As above so below" is true, then we are also here to nourish God. This is a Rune that calls for a deep probing of the meaning of profit and gain in your life. Look with care to know whether it is wealth and possessions you require for your well-being, or rather self-rule and the growth of a will.

Another concern of *Fehu* is with conserving what has already been gained. It urges vigilance and continual mindfulness, especially in times of good fortune, for it is then that we are likely to collapse ourselves into our success on the one hand, or to behave recklessly on the other. Enjoy your good fortune and remember to share it; the mark of a well-nourished self is the ability to nourish others.

Reversed: There may be considerable frustration in your life if you draw this Rune Reversed, a wide range of dispossessions reaching from the trivial to the severe: you fall short in your efforts, you reach out and miss, you get on the wrong train. You may have to sit helplessly by and watch while what you've gained starts to dwindle away. Observe what is happening. Examine the negativity from an open perspective and ask, "What lesson do I need to learn from this in my life?"

Even if there is occasion for joy, do not be seduced into mindless joyousness. Reversed, *Fehu* indicates that doubtful situations are abundant and come in many forms and guises. You are being put in touch with the shadow side of possessions. Yet all this is part of the coming to be and passing away, and is not that which abides. In dealing with the shadow side, you have an opportunity to recognize where your true nourishment lies.

12

Joy

Light

Wunjo

This Rune is a fruit-bearing branch. The term of travail is ended and you have "come to yourself" in some regard. The shift that was due has occurred and now you can freely receive its blessings, whether they be in material gain, in your emotional life or in a heightened sense of your own well-being. This is an alchemical moment in which understanding is transmuted from knowledge. The knowledge itself was a necessary but not sufficient condition; now you can rejoice, having been carried across the gap by the Tao, the Holy Spirit.

Joyousness accompanies new energy, energy blocked before now. Light pierces the clouds and touches the waters just as something lovely emerges from the depths. The soul is illuminated from within, at the meeting place of Heaven and Earth, the meeting of the waters.

There is a new clarity, which may call for you to renounce existing plans, ambitions, goals. It is proper and timely that you submit, for *Wunjo* is a

Rune of restoration, of the self properly aligned to the Self.

Reversed: Things are slow in coming to fruition. The process of birth is long and arduous, and fears arise for the safety of the "child" within. A crisis, a difficult passage—even if brief—is at hand. Consideration and deliberation are called for, because light and shadow are still intermixed and doubts and scruples might interfere with joyousness if not understood as timely to your growth. So stop your anxiety and ask yourself whether you possess the virtues of seriousness, sincerity and emptiness; to possess them is to have the tranquility that is the ground for clarity, patience and perseverance.

Seen in its true light, *everything is a test.* And so, focused in the present, sincere toward others and trusting in your process, know that you cannot fail.

This Rune Reversed is a useful meditation.

Harvest
Fertile Season
One Year

Jera

This is a Rune of beneficial outcomes. It applies to any activity or endeavor to which you are committed. Receiving this Rune encourages you to keep your spirits up. Be aware, however, that no quick results can be expected. Always a span of time is involved; hence the key words "one year," symbolizing a full cycle of time before the reaping, the harvest or deliverance.

You have prepared the ground and planted the seed. Now you must cultivate with care. To those whose labor has a long season, a long coming to term, it offers encouragement of success. Know that the outcome is in the keeping of Providence. *Jera* is a counsel to persevere.

Remember the farmer who was so eager to assist his crops that he went out at night and tugged on the new shoots. There is no way to push the river; equally you cannot hasten the harvest. Be mindful that patience is essential for the recognition of your own process, which in its season leads to the harvest of the self.

Opening
Fire
Torch

Kano

This is the Rune of opening up, of renewed clarity, of dispelling the darkness that has been shrouding some part of your life. You are free now to receive, and to know the joy of non-attached giving.

Kano is the Rune for the morning of activities, for seriousness, clarity and concentration, all of which are essential at the beginning of work. The protection offered by this Rune is that the more light you have, the better you can see what is trivial and outmoded in your conditioning.

In relationships, there can now be a mutual opening up. You may serve as the trigger, the time-keeper, through your awareness that the light of understanding is once again available to you both.

Recognize that, while on the one hand you are limited and dependent, on the other you exist at the perfect center where the harmonious and beneficent forces of the universe merge and radiate. You *are* that center.

Simply put, if you have been operating in the dark, there is now enough light to see that the patient on the operating table is yourself.

Reversed: Expect a darkening of the light in some situation or relationship. A friendship may be dying, a partnership, a marriage, some aspect of yourself, an old way of being that is no longer appropriate or valid. Receiving this Rune puts you on notice that failure to face up to the death consciously would constitute a loss of opportunity. *Kano* is one of the Cycle Runes. Reversed, it points to the death of a way of life invalidated by growth.

Reversed, this Rune calls for giving up, gladly, the old, and being prepared to live for a time empty; it calls for developing inner stability—not being seduced by the momentum of old ways while waiting for the new to become illuminated in its proper time.

15

Warrior Energy
The God Tīw

Teiwaz

This is the Rune of the Spiritual Warrior. Always the battle of the Spiritual Warrior is with the self. Funding a will through action, yet unattached to outcomes, remaining mindful that all you can really do is stay out of your own way and let the Will of Heaven flow through you—these are the hallmarks of the Spiritual Warrior.

Embodied in this Rune is the energy of discrimination, the swordlike quality that enables us to cut away the old, the dead, the extraneous. With this Rune comes the certain knowledge that the universe always has the first move. Patience is the virtue of this Rune, and it recalls for us the words of St. Augustine that "The reward of patience is patience." The molding of character is the issue when this Rune appears in your spread.

Here, you are asked to look within, to delve down to the foundations of your life itself. Only in so doing can you hope to deal with the deepest needs of your nature and to tap into your most profound resources. Associated with the Rune are the sun, yang energy, the active principle. The urge toward conquest is prominent here, especially self-conquest, which is a lifelong pursuit and calls for awareness, single-mindedness and the willingness to undergo your passage without anxiety and in total trust.

When *Teiwaz* comes in response to a question about romantic attachment, it indicates that the relationship is both timely and providential. The bond is to a partner with whom you resonate; there is work for you to do together.

If the issue relates to your devotion to a cause, an idea, a path of conduct, the Warrior Rune counsels perseverance, although, at times, the kind of perseverance called for is patience. What are your priorities? How are you using your energy? *Teiwaz* is a Rune of courage and dedication. In ancient times it was this glyph that warriors painted on their shields before battle. Now, with more refined energies in play, the same symbol strengthens your resolve in the struggle of the Self with the self.

Reversed: The danger is that through hasty or ill-timed action energy leaks out, is spilled away. If an association is short-lived, do not grieve, but know that it has fulfilled its span. Matters of trust and confidence are at issue here, and with them the authenticity of your way of being in the world.

There is a risk of collapsing into your emotions or of behaving recklessly. This is a Rune of powerful energy. Reversed, it calls for having a serious think with yourself. Examine your motives. Are you trying to dominate another? Are you focused on outcomes rather than on the activity for its own sake?

This is not a matter on which to seek outside advice. Keep your own counsel. Through consulting the Runes, you are consulting the Self, which is the action proper to a Spiritual Warrior.

16

Berkana

Growth
Rebirth
A Birch Tree

The Rune of life process, another of the Cycle Runes, *Berkana* denotes that form of fertility that promotes growth both symbolically and actually. The growth may occur in affairs of the world, family matters, one's relationship to one's Self or to the Divine. This is a "leading to" Rune in that it leads to blossoming and ripening.

What is called for here is going into things deeply, with care and awareness. This Rune is concerned with the power of influencing development and with the flow of beings into their new forms. Its action is gentle and penetrating and pervasive.

First disperse resistance, then accomplish the work. For this to happen, your will must be clear and controlled. In regard to the issue, your motives must be correct. Any "dark corners" should be cleansed; this must be carried out diligently and sometimes with expert help. Modesty, patience, fairness and generosity are called for here. Do you possess these virtues? Once resistance is dispersed and rectification carried out and seen to hold firm, then through steadfastness and right attitude, the blossoming can occur.

Reversed: Events or, more likely, aspects of character, interfere with the growth of new life and life process. You may feel dismay at failing to take right action. But rather than dismay, what is called for here is diligence. Examine what has taken place, your role in it, your needs, the needs of others. Are you placing your *wants* before the *needs* of others? Strip down until you can identify the blocks to growth in this situation. Then, penetrating gently, imitate the wind.

You may be required to fertilize the ground again; but through correct preparation, growth is assured.

17

Movement

Progress

A Horse

Ehwaz

The Rune of movement, of physical shifts, new dwelling places, new attitudes, new life; movement, also, in the sense of improving or bettering any situation. *Ehwaz* is a Rune of transit and transition.

There is about this Rune a sense of gradual development and steady progress, with the accompanying notion of slow growth through numerous shifts and changes. This could apply to the growth of a business or to the development of an idea. A relationship also needs to undergo changes and transformations if it is to maintain growth and life. Personal moral effort and persevering steadfastness are called for when you draw this Rune.

Let it be said this way: "As I cultivate my nature, all else follows." A horse is the Rune-symbol because it progresses gradually. From Bronze Age artifacts we find the sun linked to the horse; the horse both symbolized the sun and was regarded as drawing it across the sky. Here, this Rune is saying, you have progressed far enough to feel a measure of safety, of surety in your position. Now, it is time to turn again and face the future reassured and prepared to share the good fortune that comes. This last, the sharing, is significant, as it relates to the power of the sun to foster life and illuminate all things in its light.

Reversed: Movement that appears to block. This Rune Reversed puts you on notice that an opportunity is at hand and should not be ignored. Be certain that what you are doing—or not doing—is timely. There are no missed opportunities; we have simply to recognize that all opportunities are *not* for us, all possibilities are *not* open to us. If you are feeling at a loss, unclear about the need to act, consider what is timely and appropriate to your nature: the opportunity at hand may be precisely to avoid action. Remember that what is yours will come to you.

18

Flow
Water

Laguz

That Which Conducts

The urge toward unconsciousness, toward the past and immersion in the flow of feeling, toward the mother, the womb's security—all this is inherent in this Rune. Unseen powers are active here, creative and fertile powers of Nature. The attributes of *Laguz* are water, fluidity, the ebb and flow of tides and emotions, careers and relationships. It fulfills our need to immerse ourselves in the experience of living without having to evaluate or understand, it speaks to the desire for comfort and the satisfaction of emotional needs, the lunar side of our nature. For while the sun strives for differentiation, the moon draws us toward unity and merging.

This Rune often signals a time for cleansing: for revaluing, reorganizing, realigning. A Rune of knowing and psychic power, it may call you to study spiritual matters in readiness for deep self-transformation. For a man, success now lies in contacting his intuitive knowing; for a woman, in attuning to her own rhythms. A Rune of the self relating rightly to the Self, it signifies what alchemists called the *conjunctio,* or sacred marriage. In fairy tales, it is the end where the hero and heroine live happily ever after.

Reversed: A warning against overreach, excessive striving; a counsel against trying to exceed your own strength or operate beyond the power you have funded to date in your life.

This Rune Reversed often indicates a failure to draw upon the wisdom of instinct. As a result, the intuitive side of your nature may be languishing, leaving you permanently out of balance. What is called for now is to go within, to honor the receptive side of your Warrior Nature.

19

Disruptive Natural Forces
Elemental Power

Hagalaz

Hail

The urge for change, freedom, invention and liberation invest this Rune. Drawing it indicates a pressing need within the psyche to break free from constricting identification with material reality and to experience the world of archetypal mind.

Hagalaz is the Rune of elemental disruption, of events totally beyond your control. Although it has only an Upright position, it always operates through reversal. When you draw this Rune, expect disruption of your plans, for it is the great "Awakener," although the form the awakening takes may vary. Perhaps you will experience a gradual feeling of coming to your senses, as though you were emerging from a long sleep. Then again, the onset of power may be such as to rip away the fabric of what you previously knew as your reality, your security, your understanding of yourself, your work, your relationships and beliefs.

Be aware, however, that what operates here is not ultimately an outside force, not a situation of you-at-the-mercy-of-externals. Your own nature is creating what's happening, and you are not without power in this situation. The inner strength you have funded until now in your life is your support and guide at a time when everything you've taken for granted is being challenged.

Receiving this Rune puts you on notice: you may sustain loss or damage—a tree falls on your home, a relationship fails, plans go wrong, a source of supply dries up. But you are forewarned and, therefore, encouraged to understand and accept what occurs as necessary, called for in your deeps out of a pressing need for growth.

There is nothing trivial about this Rune. The more severe the disruption in your life, the more significant and timely the requirements for your growth. The term "radical discontinuity" best describes the action of this, another of the Cycle Runes, at its most forceful: the universe and your own soul are demanding that you do, indeed, grow.

20

A Journey
Communication
Union, Reunion

Raido

This Rune is concerned with communication, with the attunement of something that has two sides, two elements, and with the ultimate reunion that comes as the end of the journey when what is above and what is below are united and of one mind. The journey is the soul's journey. Moreover, the approach of that which is above and that which is below is realized from inmost sentiment rather than through the force of circumstances. A simple prayer for the soul's journey is:

I will to will Thy will.

Such a simple form of prayer is proper, it seems, on almost any occasion. It is a suitable preamble, in particular, to healing. *Raido* is another of the Runes in the Cycle of Self-Transformation.

Inner worth mounts here, and at such a time we must remember that we are not intended to rely entirely upon our own power, but instead to ask what is right action. Ask through prayer, through addressing your own knowing, your body knowing, the Witness Self, the Teacher Within. Once you are clear, then you can neutralize your refusal to let right action flow through you. Not intent on movement, be content to wait. While you wait, keep on removing resistances. As the obstructions give way, all remorse arising from "trying to make it happen" disappears.

As always, the journey is toward self-healing, self-change and union. You are concerned here with nothing less than unobstructed, perfect union. But the union of Heaven and Earth cannot be forced. Keep within your limits. Regulate any excesses in your life. Material advantages must *not* weigh heavily on this journey of the self toward the Self.

Trust your own Process—that is the essence of this Rune. Keep on cutting away illusions. Stand apart even from like-minded others; the notion of strength in numbers does not apply at this time, for this part of the journey cannot be shared. Innermost feeling, spontaneously expressed, is the only right action now. This Rune urges you to undertake your journey, your quest—and if you have already begun, to continue.

Reversed: Receiving this Rune Reversed puts you on notice to be particularly attentive to personal relationships. At this time, ruptures are more likely than reconciliations. Effort will be required on your part. Keep your good humor; whatever happens, how you *respond* is up to you.

The requirements of your process may totally disrupt what you had intended. Hoped-for outcomes may elude you. And yet what you regard as detours, inconveniences, disruptions, blockages and even failures and deaths will actually be *rerouting opportunities,* with union and reunion as the only abiding destinations.

Gateway
Place of Non–Action

Thurisaz

With a gateway for its symbol, this Rune indicates that there is work to be done both inside and outside yourself. The Spirit of Transformation guards the gate of the personal world, looking out as well as in, symbolizing the abiding urge to transcend the limits of the little self. The gateway is at once a portal and a frontier between Heaven and the mundane. Arriving here is a recognition of your readiness to contact the numinous, the Divine, to illuminate your experience so that its meaning shines through its form.

Thurisaz is a Rune of non-action. The gateway is not to be approached and passed through without contemplation. Here you are being confronted with a true reflection of what is hidden in yourself, what must be exposed and examined before successful action can be undertaken. This Rune's strength lies in its ability to wait. This is not a time to take decisions. Deep transformational forces are at work in this next to last of the Cycle Runes.

Visualize a gateway on a hilltop. Your entire life lies behind you and below. Before you pass through, pause and review the past: the learning and the joys, the tests and tribulations, all that it took to bring you here. Bless it, and release it all. For in so doing you reclaim what is truly yours—your power in the universe.

Step through the gateway now.

Reversed: Correct conduct is based on right attitude. If, indeed, you are undergoing difficulties, remember that *the quality of your passage is up to you.* Be certain that you are not suffering over your suffering. Once again, consider the uses of adversity.

Hasty decisions at this time may cause regrets, for the probability is that you will act from weakness, deceive yourself about your motives and create new problems more severe than those you are attempting to resolve. Impulses must be tempered by thought for correct procedure. Keep still and collect yourself, wait on the Tao, the Will of Heaven— nothing else is timely now. Do not attempt to go beyond where you haven't yet begun.

Enforced contemplation is the essence of this Rune Reversed. Drawing it indicates a quickening of your development. Yet even when the growth process accelerates there will be halts along the way to reconsider, to integrate. Take advantage of these halts.

22

Breakthrough
Transformation
Day

Dagaz

Here is the final Rune belonging to the Cycle of Self-Transformation. Drawing it marks a major shift or breakthrough in the process of self-change, a complete transformation in attitude—a 180-degree turn. For some, the transition is so radical that they no longer continue to live the ordinary life in the ordinary way.

Because the timing is right, the outcome is assured although not, from the present vantage point, predictable. Rely, therefore, on radical trust, even though the moment may call for you to leap, empty-handed, into the void. Confront and vanquish your refusal to let right action flow through you. In each life there comes at least one moment which, if recognized and seized, transforms the course of that life forever. With this Rune your Warrior Nature reveals itself.

If *Dagaz* is followed by the Blank Rune, the magnitude of the transformation might be so total as to portend a death, the successful conclusion to your passage.

A major period of achievement and prosperity is sometimes introduced by this Rune. The darkness is behind you; daylight has come. However, as always, you are put on notice to be mindful not to collapse yourself into the future or to behave recklessly in your new situation. A lot of hard work can be involved in a time of transformation. Undertake to do it joyfully.

23

Standstill
That Which Impedes
Ice

Isa

The winter of the spiritual life is upon you. You may find yourself entangled in a situation to whose implications you are, in effect, blind. You may be powerless to do anything except submit, surrender, even sacrifice some long-cherished desire. Be patient, for this is the fallow period that precedes a rebirth.

Positive accomplishment is unlikely now. There is a freeze on useful activity, all your plans on hold. You may be experiencing an unaccustomed drain on your energy and wonder why: the chill wind is reaching you over the ice floes of old outmoded habits.

Trying to hold on can result in shallowness of feeling, a sense of being out of touch with life, out of phase. Seek to discover what it is you are holding onto that keeps this condition in effect, and let go. Shed, release, cleanse away the old. That will bring on the thaw. Usually *Isa* requires a sacrifice of the personal, the "I."

And yet there is no reason for anxiety. Submit

113

and be still, for what you are experiencing is not necessarily the result of your actions, your habits, but of the conditions of the time, against which you can do nothing. What has been full must empty; what has increased must decrease. This is the way of Heaven and Earth. To surrender is to display courage and wisdom.

At such a time, do not hope to rely on help or friendly support. Exercise caution in your isolation, and do not stubbornly persist in attempting to work your will. Remain mindful that the seed of the new is present in the shell of the old, the seed of unrealized potential, the seed of the good. Your conduct now will bring the new fruit to ripeness, or cause it to rot on the vine. Trust your own process, and watch for signs of spring.

24

Wholeness
Life Forces
The Sun's Energy

Sowelu

The symbol of this Rune is wholeness, that which our nature requires. It embodies the impulse toward self-realization and indicates the path you must follow, not from ulterior motives but from the essence of your individuality.

Seeking after wholeness is the heart of the Warrior's quest. And yet what you are striving to become in actuality is what you already are in essence: it is your *personal myth,* that which you are to make conscious, bring into form, express in a creative way. The sun symbolizes the path and illuminates the goal, which is the human heart.

A Rune of great power, making life force available to you, *Sowelu* marks a time for recharging and regeneration right down to the cellular level. You may actually experience power surges, for the energies involved can be drastic. Although this Rune has no Reversed position, there is reason for caution. You may even see fit to withdraw, to retreat in the face of a pressing situation, especially if events or people are demanding that you "spend" your energy now. Know that such a retreat is a retreat in strength, and that it can mark a voyage inward for centering, for balance. Timely retreat is among the skills of the Spiritual Warrior.

At the same time, for some, this Rune counsels opening yourself up, letting the Light into some part of your life that has been secret, shut away. To accomplish this may call for profound recognitions, for admitting to yourself something that you have long denied. There is a prayer known as the *Gayatri* that embodies the spirit of this Rune. Address the sun in this fashion:

> *You, who are the source of all power,*
> *Whose rays illuminate the whole world,*
> *Illuminate also my heart*
> *So that it too can do your work.*

While reciting the *Gayatri*, visualize the sun's rays streaming forth into the world, entering your own heart, and then streaming out of your heart center in turn. This is an extremely powerful and life-enhancing prayer.

Again, there is a caution not to give yourself airs. Yet, even in a time of bountiful energy, you are required to face and vanquish your refusal to let right action flow through you. Nourish this capacity, for it is your true function. Aim yourself truly and maintain your aim without manipulation.

Practice the art of not forcing. Aim yourself

truly and then maintain your aim without manipulative effort. Meditate on Christ's words: *I can of mine own self do nothing.* For in our own power, we do nothing; even in loving, it is Love that loves through us. This way of thinking and being integrates new energies and permits you to flow into wholeness, which is the ultimate realization of your personal myth, and the goal of the Spiritual Warrior.

The Unknowable
The Blank Rune

Odin

Blank is the end, blank the beginning. This is the Rune of total trust and should be taken as exciting evidence of your most immediate contact with your own true destiny which, time and again, rises like the phoenix from the ashes of what we call fate.

Odin can portend a death. But that death is usually symbolic, and may relate to any part of your life as you are living it now. Relinquishing control is the ultimate challenge for the Spiritual Warrior.

Here the Unknowable informs you that it is in motion in your life. In that blankness is held undiluted potential. At the same time pregnant and empty, it comprehends the totality of being, all that is to be actualized.

Drawing the Blank Rune brings to the surface our deepest fears: Will I fail? Will I be abandoned? Will it all be taken away? And yet, within that blankness is held our highest good, our truest possibilities and all our fertile dreams.

Willingness and permitting are what this Rune

requires, for how can you exercise control over what is not yet in form? And what is coming to be can never arise from the known. Once again, this Rune often calls for no less an act of courage than the empty-handed leap into the void. Drawing it is a direct test of Faith.

If karma is the sum total of what you have done, the limits on what you are and will become, then it may be useful to see in this Rune the path of karma. Yet from the runic perspective, even the very debts of old karma shift and evolve as you shift and evolve. *Nothing is predestined;* there is nothing that cannot be avoided. And if, indeed, there are "matters hidden by the gods," you need only remember: what beckons is the creative power of the unknown.

Whenever this Rune appears in your spread, take heart: it is the source from which flows the energy for self-change. Know that the work of self-transformation is progressing in your life.

7

AFTERWORD:
MAGIC IN THE
PRESENT TENSE

God is alive, magic is afoot.

Buffy Sainte-Marie

The Runes are available to be used as a bridge to your Knowing Self. While contemplating a Rune chosen to illuminate a particular issue, remain clear about one thing: *you are not depending on the Oracle to solve your problems for you.* Images and thoughts will come to mind, image-ideas that will provide you with the necessary clues as to what constitutes timely right action. Working with the Oracle in this way, you will fund a new sense of confidence, a new kind of courage.

The Viking Runes, then, are a mirror for the magic of our Knowing Selves. They are magical play and sacred play. In time, as you become skilled in their use, you can perhaps lay the Runes aside and permit the knowing to arise unfiltered, just as some dowsers use only their bare hands. Tuning in directly to the Self is owning your own power as a Co-creator, and that is the ultimate "magic" toward which this world is tending, toward which the rivers of awareness flow.

Any Oracle is a reflection of the culture in which it evolves. The roots of the Tarot and the *I Ching* are not Western roots; the Tarot did not emerge into Western life until the Runes were more than 1,000 years old; the *I Ching* took another 800 years to reach us. In the Runes we are provided with a symbolic system that derives from our own consciousness, an Oracle arising within the forms of Western thought. All this makes the Viking Runes uniquely ours. Thus it seems to me both timely and providential that the Runes once again be restored to service as a truly Western Oracle.

To all of you who have arrived at this place of "termination and new beginnings," *Gud blessi thig.*

SELECTED BIBLIOGRAPHY

Bonner, W. "Survivals of Paganism in Anglo-Saxon England." *Transactions of the Birmingham Archaeological Society*, vol. 56, 1932.

Branston, B. *The Lost Gods of England.* London, 1957.

Dickens, B. "English Names and Old English Heathenism." *Essays and Studies*, vol. 19, 1934.

———. "Runic Rings and Old English Charms." *Archiv Stud. neuren Sprachen*, vol. 167, 1935.

———. "A System of Transliteration for Old English Runic Inscriptions." *Leeds Studies in English*, vol. 1, 1932.

Elliott, Ralph W. V. *Runes: An Introduction.* Manchester, Eng.: Manchester University Press, 1959.

———. "Runes, Yews, and Magic." *Speculum*, vol. 32, 1957.

Grattan, J.H.G., and Singer, S. *Anglo-Saxon Magic and Medicine.* London, 1952.

Haugen, Einar. *The Scandinavian Languages.* Cambridge, Mass.: Harvard University Press, 1976.

Hermannsson, H. Catalogue of Runic Literature—Part of the Icelandic Collection Bequeathed by Willard Fiske. Cornell University Library.

Hollander, Lee M. *The Poetic Edda.* Austin: University of Texas Press, 1964.

Howard, Michael. *The Magic of the Runes.* New York: Samuel Weiser, 1980.

————. *The Runes and Other Magical Alphabets.* Wellingborough, Northants, Eng.: Aquarian Press, 1978.

Jansson, Sven B. F. *The Runes of Sweden.* Translated by Peter Foote. London: Phoenix House, 1962.

Jones, Gwyn. *History of the Vikings.* London: Oxford University Press, 1968.

Knoop, Douglas, and Jones, G. P. *The Mediaeval Mason.* Manchester, Eng.: Manchester University Press, 1967.

Krause, Wolfgang. *Was Mann in Runen Ritzte.* Halle, Ger.: M. Niemeyer, 1935.

Marstrander, C.J.S. "Om runene og runenavnenes oprindelse." *Norsk tidsskrift for sprogvidenskap,* vol. 1, 1928.

Napier, A. S. "The Franks Casket." *An English Miscellany Presented to Dr. Furnwall.* London: Oxford University Press, 1901.

Page, R. I. *An Introduction to English Runes,* London: Methuen, 1973.

Ravenscroft, Trevor. *The Spear of Destiny.* London: Neville Spearman, 1972.

Souers, P. W. *Harvard Studies and Notes in Philology and Literature,* vol. 17, 1935; vol. 18, 1936; vol. 19, 1937.

Spiesberger, Karl. *Runenmagie, Handbuch der Runenkunde.* Berlin: Richard Schikowski, 1955.

Stephens, G. *Handbook of the Old-Northern Runic Monuments of Scandinavia and England.* London and Copenhagen, 1884.

————. *The Old-Northern Runic Monuments of Scandinavia and England.* London and Copenhagen, 1866–1901.

Storms, G. *Anglo-Saxon Magic.* The Hague, 1948.

Taylor, I. *Greeks and Goths: A Study on the Runes.* London, 1879.

Thompson, Claiborne W. *Studies in Upplandic Runography.* Austin: University of Texas Press, 1975.

Walgren, Erik. *The Kensington Rune Stone: A Mystery Solved.* Madison: University of Wisconsin Press, 1958.

Wimmer, L.F.A. "Runeskriftens Oprindelse og Udvikling i Norden." *Aaboger for nordisk Oldkyndighed og Historie,* 1874.

GUIDES TO THE TRANSFORMATIONAL PROCESS

A Course in Miracles. Foundation for Inner Peace, P.O. Box 635, Tiburon, CA 94920.

Brenner, Paul. *Life Is a Shared Creation.* Marina del Rey, CA: De-Vorss, 1981.

Chancellor, Philip, ed. *Handbook of the Bach Flower Remedies.* Saffron Walden, Eng.: C.W. Daniel Co., 1971

Daily Word. a pamphlet issued monthly from Unity Village, MO 64065.

Dass, Ram. *The Only Dance There Is.* Garden City, NY: Anchor Books, 1974.

Epictetus. *The Enchiridion.* Translated by Thomas W. Higginson. Indianapolis: Bobbs-Merrill, 1980.

Ferguson, Marilyn. *The Aquarian Conspiracy.* Los Angeles: Tarcher, 1980.

Frydman, Maurice, translator. *I Am That: Conversations with Sri Nisargadatta Maharaj,* Parts I and II. Durham, NC: Acorn Press, 1973.

Gendlin, Eugene T. *Focusing.* New York: Bantam, 1981.

Gibran, Kahlil. *The Prophet.* New York: Knopf, 1980.

Greene, Liz. *Relating: An Astrological Guide to Living with Others on a Small Planet.* London: Coventure, 1977.

Joy, W. Brugh. *Joy's Way: A Map for the Transformational Journey.* Los Angeles: Tarcher, 1979.

Jung, C. J. *Memories, Dreams, and Reflections.* New York: Pantheon, 1961.

Keyes, Laurel Elizabeth. *Toning: The Creative Power of the Voice.* Marina del Rey, CA: DeVorss, 1973.

Lao Tzu. *Tao Te Ching.* Translated by Gia-Fu Feng and Jane English. New York: Vintage Books, 1972.

Leonard, George. *The Silent Pulse: A Search for the Perfect Rhythm That Exists in Each of Us.* New York: Bantam, 1981.

Levine, Stephen. *Who Dies?* An Investigation of Conscious Living and Conscious Dying. New York: Anchor Books, 1982.

Musashi, Miyamoto. *A Book of Five Rings: The Classic Guide to Strategy.* Woodstock, NY: Overlook Press, 1974.

Rainwater, Janette. *You're in Charge.* Los Angeles: Guild of Tutors Press, 1979.

Spangler, David. *Emergence: The Rebirth of the Sacred.* New York: Delacorte, 1984.

Star + Gate, a Symbolic System. Available from Cloud Enterprises, P.O. Box 1006, Orinda, CA 94563. (The American Tarot.)

THE NEW ORACLE FOUNDATION

The Viking Runes—what comes next?

Developing a rewarding interaction with one's own private Rune Oracle has been, for many people, an exciting adventure in self-discovery. I would be most interested to hear of *your* experiences with The Viking Runes. Please feel free to write to me at The New Oracle Foundation.

Learning how to tap into the "magic" properties of the subconcious Knowing Mind places one amongst a very special group of people who have also experienced this aspect of their own potential abilities. We now need some way to establish better contact with each other and thereby to stimulate further mutual growth along the path of the Spiritual Warrior. To this end, I am developing the New Oracle Foundation that will publish a quarterly newsletter, *The New Oracle News.* This newsletter will serve as a forum for all of us to share our experiences with The Viking Runes. It will contain insights into the oracular tradition, innovations in Rune-casting techniques, and new aspects of "Rune play" discovered by readers of *The Book of Runes;* and will, in addition, serve as the source for new product information, ranging from crystal Rune pendants to computer programs for Rune play.

For further information as to Foundation membership, and to receive *The New Oracle News* for one year, send a five dollar donation to cover costs of publication and mailing to:

The New Oracle Foundation
45–454 Ihilani Street
Kaneohe, Hawaii   96744

ABOUT THE AUTHOR

Ralph Blum received his degree in Russian studies at Harvard. Following a period in Italy as a Fulbright Scholar he returned to Harvard where he did graduate work in anthropology with grants from the National Science Foundation and the Ford Foundation. He is a writer and a publisher.

Blum is the author of three novels. His nonfiction book, *Beyond Earth—Man's Contact with UFOs*, was written in collaboration with Judy Blum and is recognized as a major contribution to the field. It has over 800,000 copies in print.

Futhark (*Traditional Order*)

MODERN ENGLISH LETTER	OLD ENGLISH RUNES	OLD ENGLISH NAMES	GERMANIC RUNES	GERMANIC NAMES	ETRUSCAN	PRE-RUNIC SYMBOLS
f	ᚠ	feoh	ᚠ	fehu	ʅ	
u	ᚢ	ūr	ᚢ	ūruz	Y V	Δ
þ(th)	ᚦ	þorn	ᚦ	þurisaz		
a	ᚼ	ōs	ᚨ	ansuz	A	
r	ᚱ	rād	ᚱ	raiðō	◁	
k	ᚳ	cēn	<	kaunaz kēnaz kanō	>X	
g	ᚷ	gyfu	ᚷ	gebō		X
w	ᚹ	wyn	ᚹ	wunjō		
h	ᚻ	haegl	ᚺ	hagalaz	⍭	目
n	ᚾ	nȳð	ᚾ	nauþiz	Υ (ł)	+
i	ᛁ	īs	ᛁ	īsa-	I	I
j	ᛄ	gēr	ᛃ	jēra-		ↄ
e (ei)	ᛇ	ēoh	ᛇ	eihwaz		⯑ ⯑
p	ᛈ	peorð	ᛈ	perþ	◁	
z	ᛉ	eolh-secg	ᛉ	algiz	I ‡	Y Ӝ
s	ᛋ	sigel	<	sowelu	≷	
t	ᛏ	tīr	ᛏ	teiwaz	Τ Χ	↑ ↑
b	ᛒ	beorc	ᛒ	berkana-		
e	ᛖ	e(o)h	ᛖ	ehwaz	⅃	
m	ᛗ	man	ᛗ	mannaz ·	m ᛘ	⌒
l	ᛚ	lagu	ᛚ	laguz	↓	
ng	ᛝ	Ing	□	inguz	φ	□ φ
ð	◇	daeg	ᛞ	ðagaz		Χ Χ
o	ᛟ	eþel	ᛟ	oþila		ᛟ

Note: While the order of Rune names was to some degree fortuitous, the choice of names was not. A Rune name had to begin with a given sound and possess mnemonic power.